Including and Supporting Preschool Children with Developmental Delays in Early Childhood Programs

Editors:

William H. Brown
University of South Carolina

Maureen A. Conroy
University of Florida

SOUTHERN
EARLY
CHILDHOOD
ASSOCIATION

7107 W. 12th St., Ste. 102 • Little Rock, AR 72204
P.O. Box 55930 • Little Rock, AR 72215-5930
Office: **501-663-0353** • FAX: **501-663-2114**

Southern Early Childhood Association
P.O. Box 55930
Little Rock, AR 72215-5930

Copyright © 1997 by Southern Early Childhood Association
All rights reserved. No part of this book may be reproduced in
any form or by electronic or mechanical means, including information
storage and retrieval systems, without permission in writing from
the publisher, except by a reviewer, who may quote brief passages
in a review.

The names of all children and families in this book have been changed to protect
their privacy.

The Southern Early Childhood Association provides a variety of publications,
videos, and symposia for teachers and care givers of young children. For more
information about our services, write, call, or e-mail us at SECA@aristotle.net or
visit us on the Internet at www.seca50.org.

SECA makes every effort to assure that developmentally appropriate practices
and cultural diversity are depicted throughout our publications, products, and
materials. The opinions expressed in this book, however, are those of the
author(s) and not necessarily of SECA and/or its affiliates.

ISBN 0-942388-22-4

Printed in the United States of America
by A.C.H. Graphics   tel. 1-501-753-6113

This book is dedicated to
Carson Nicholas Mosso (d.o.b. 5/8/91),
who has taught me more about early childhood
than any of my professional colleagues or the
many books I have read concerning the subject.

About the Editors—

William H. Brown, Ph.D., is an assistant professor of Special Education in the Department of Educational Psychology and Early Childhood Education at the University of South Carolina. His current professional interest includes: early intervention for infants, toddlers, preschoolers, and young children who are developmentally delayed or are at high risk for being developmentally delayed, abused and neglected, and behavior disordered. During his twenty-three-year professional career, he has also been a parent trainer, a service coordinator, a director of a large early intervention program, and a consultant with community preschool programs. His six-year-old son, Carson Nicholas Mosso, is a first grader at North Springs Elementary in Columbia.

Maureen A. Conroy, Ph.D., is an assistant professor in the Department of Special Education at the University of Florida. Her current professional interests include research and instruction in early intervention with emphasis on young children with developmental disabilities and behavioral challenges. She has been involved in the field of early intervention for eighteen years as a teacher of children with developmental delays, as a consultant to Head Start and early intervention programs, as an administrator to early intervention programs, and as a parent and university-level teacher trainer. Maureen presents at numerous professional conferences on early intervention.

Foreword

This book is intended to be a resource for Early Childhood Educators...

Twenty years ago, M. J. Guralnick (1978) as the editor and his many co-authors could write a single book that covered the information known about the inclusion of young children in early childhood programs. Today, however, many excellent sources of information on early childhood inclusion are available. Our goal with this book has been to provide early childhood educators with high-quality and contemporary information that they might need while serving young children with developmental delays and their families in early childhood programs. To that end, Wes Brown has presented information on family-centered services, a recommended practice in early childhood special education for over a decade now. Judy Neimyer has addressed the current need for collaboration in high-quality inclusive early childhood programs. Julian Cripe and Julia Lee have outlined the basic principles of activity-based intervention strategies for working with young children with and without development delays in early childhood settings. Maureen Conroy and William Brown have presented contemporary intervention strategies for promoting children's language in inclusive early childhood programs. William Brown and Maureen Conroy have delineated a model for promoting and supporting the social development of young children with and without developmental delays. Finally, Ana Lopez Defede and Janice Weber have addressed the emerging assistive technologies that can be employed with young children with and without developmental delays in preschool settings. We sincerely hope that readers find the information contained in the book helpful to them professionally as they work with young children and their families.

We want to sincerely thank all the contributing authors for their time and effort in writing their respective chapters. All the authors have incredibly busy schedules and were diligent in responding to our editorial concerns and in completing their contributions to the book. In addition, we want to thank Clarissa Willis, Executive Director of SECA, for her able assistance in bringing this book to completion. Without her supportive "behind the scene efforts" and her periodic encouragement (and reminders), the quality of this book would have suffered greatly.

Editors:

William H. Brown
University of South Carolina
Maureen A. Conroy
University of Florida

Introduction

Almost twenty-five years ago, Betty Caldwell (1973) discussed three major evolutionary trends in the history of serving young children with developmental delays. She noted that before the 1950s societal attitudes toward individuals with disabilities were characterized by "forgetting and hiding" them. Until the deinstitutionalization movements of the 1950s and 1960s, many children with developmental delays were either hidden away in their homes or "warehoused" in large, depersonalizing institutional facilities. During the 1950s and 1960s, Caldwell noted a second evolutionary trend marked by initial societal attempts to systematically promote the well being of children with developmental delays. Unfortunately, most of these initial efforts were focused on establishing and maintaining segregated special education programs for children with developmental delays. Hence, Caldwell characterized the second evolutionary period as a time of "screening and segregating" young children with developmental delays. Finally, Caldwell noted a third evolutionary trend in the 1970s in which society began in earnest "identifying and helping" young children with developmental delays and their families. The societal actions and commitments of the 1970s resulted in the further development of early childhood special education programs for young children with developmental delays in many communities throughout the nation.

The proliferation of early childhood special education services was greatly promoted by the passage of landmark legislation that mandated a "free and appropriate education" (FAPE) in "the least restrictive environment (LRE) for children with disabilities in the 1970s and 1980s (i.e., *Public Laws 94-142* and *99-457*). Caldwell and other child advocates have argued that we should continue "identifying and helping" young children with developmental delays. To Caldwell's historical perspective, we want to add a fourth evolutionary trend. As advocates for young children, during the final years of the 1990s, we should promote and proactively work toward "including and supporting" young children with developmental delays and their families in their communities, particularly high-quality early childhood programs (Brown & Mosso, 1996).

Taking Stock of Where We Are with Early Childhood Inclusion

Mainstreaming, integrating, and including young children with developmental delays in programs with peers *without* developmental delays began over twenty-five years ago (e.g., Allen, Benning, & Drummond, 1972; Bricker & Bricker, 1976; Guralnick, 1978). Inclusion of young children with developmental delays in early childhood programs has had legal (e.g., *Individuals with Disabilities Education Act Public Laws 102-119* and

105-17; Americans with Disabilities Act Public Law 101-336), scientific (e.g., Buysee & Bailey, 1993; Lamorey & Bricker, 1993), and public policy support (e.g., Bredekamp & Copple, 1997; Division for Early Childhood, 1993). Researchers who have reviewed the results of early childhood inclusion have concluded that children with developmental delays who are served in high-quality inclusive preschool programs make at least as much developmental progress on critical abilities (e.g., cognitive, language, social, motor skills) as do children with developmental delays in segregated and supposedly specialized early childhood special education programs (i.e., programs with only children with special needs) (Buysee & Bailey, 1993; Lamorey & Bricker, 1993, Odom & McEvoy, 1988). Moreover, reports of difficulties for children *without* developmental delays in inclusive early childhood programs are noticeably absent from the professional literature. For example, the evaluation of a recent inclusive early childhood program that provided support services to young children with developmental delays in community child care programs revealed the following:

➡ children with developmental delays in community child care programs were as meaningfully engaged in appropriate preschool activities and had similar levels of adult support when compared to children with developmental delays in segregated early childhood special education programs;

➡ children with developmental delays in community child care programs made similar developmental progress on their individualized goals and developmental assessments when compared to children with developmental delays in segregated early childhood special education programs;

➡ children with developmental delays in community child care programs had significantly more positive interactions with peers when compared to children with developmental delays in segregated early childhood special education programs;

➡ consumer satisfaction interviews showed consistent satisfaction by parents and teachers of children with developmental delays in inclusive community child care programs; and

➡ the inclusive service delivery model was implemented at similar costs to the segregated early childhood special education programs (Brown, Horn, Heiser, & Odom, in press).

Since the passage of *Public Law 99-457* in 1986, state governments have established early intervention programs for infants and toddlers with developmental delays and their families (Smith & McKenna, 1994) and local education agencies (LEAs) have begun to provide three-, four-, and five-year-old children with disabilities with a free and appropriate education (FAPE) (Trohanis, 1994). In recent years, increasing emphasis has been placed on inclusive early intervention and early childhood education and inclusion has become a recommended practice in both early childhood special education (e.g., Bricker, Peck, & Odom, 1993; DEC Task Force on Recommended Practices, 1993; Division for

Early Childhood, 1993) and early childhood education (e.g., Wolery, Strain, & Bailey, 1992; Wolery & Wilbers, 1994). Indeed, New and Mallory (1994) noted that an ethic of inclusion, which is based on a recognition of the importance of human diversity, has emerged in early childhood education. Despite federal and state educational laws that require educational and related services (e.g., speech therapy, physical therapy) in the least restrictive environment (LRE) and recognition of inclusion as a recommended practice, inclusive early childhood programs have continued to be the exception rather than the rule in many areas of the nation, particularly for young children with significant developmental delays. For example, the most recently analyzed national information has indicated that only 48% of preschool children with developmental delays are served primarily in educational programs for young children *without* developmental delays (i.e., included in general early childhood programs) (U. S. Department of Education, 1996). The remainder of the preschool children with developmental delays are served either in separate classes or separate schools for children with special needs or at home or in residential facilities.

A Contemporary Definition of Inclusion

Although early childhood inclusion has been advocated by professionals and parents for many years, its definition has remained ambiguous. Recently, Odom and his colleagues in the Early Childhood Research Institute on Inclusion (Odom et al., 1996) provided a working definition of early childhood inclusion with four important dimensions that were derived from federal laws that have mandated educational and related services for children with disabilities in the least restrictive environment.[1] For Odom and his colleagues, the four critical characteristics of inclusion have been:

➡ the active participation of young children with and *without* developmental delays in the same community program (e.g., Head Start programs, public preschools, private child care centers and preschools);

➡ service provision with planning and collaboration of professionals from different disciplines (i.e., an interdisciplinary perspective);

➡ service provision that promotes the accomplishment of individualized goals established for children with developmental delays by a planning team consisting of parents, professionals, and paraprofessionals (i.e., a multidisciplinary team); and

➡ evaluation of the progress children with developmental delays are making toward accomplishing the individualized goals established by their multidisciplinary team.

Odom and his colleagues also noted that early childhood inclusion extends beyond preschool programs into other community and family activities (e.g., participation in church, birthday parties). Recently, Brown and Mosso (1996) defined inclusion in a relatively straightforward manner as *"...the degree to which children with developmental delays are playing, learning, working, and living with family and friends in their communities."*

This definition incorporates the four critical aspects of the Odom et al. (1996) definition of early childhood inclusion and is a practical definition for parents and professionals who are interested in early childhood inclusion.

Preparation of this introduction was supported by a Research and Productive Scholarship Grant, Wardlaw College of Education, and the Insititute for Families in Society at University of South Carolina.

References

Allen, K. E., Benning, P. M., & Drummond, W. T. (1972). Integration of normal and handicapped children in a behavior modification preschool: A case study. In G. Semp (Ed.), *Behavior analysis and education* (pp. 127-141). Lawrence, KS: University of Kansas.

Bredekamp, S., & Copple, C. (1997). Developmentally Appropriate Practice in early childhood programs serving children from birth through age 8: NAEYC Position Statement adopted July 1996. In S. Bredekamp & C. Copple (Eds.), *Developmentally Appropriate Practice in early childhood programs* (Revised Edition) (pp. 3-30). Washington, DC: National Association for the Education of Young Children.

Bricker, W. A., & Bricker, D. D. (1976). The infant, toddler, and preschool research and intervention project. In T. D. Tojossem (Ed.), *Intervention strategies for high risk infants and young children* (pp. 545-572). Baltimore: University Park Press.

Bricker, D. D., Peck, C. A., & Odom, S. L. (1993). Integration: Campaign for the new century. In C. A. Peck, S. L. Odom, & D. D. Bricker (Eds.), *Integrating young children with disabilities into community programs: Ecological perspectives on research and implementation* (pp. 271-276). Baltimore: Paul H. Brookes.

Brown, W. H., Horn, E. M., Heiser, J. G., & Odom, S. L. (in press). Project BLEND: An inclusive model of early intervention services. *Journal of Early Intervention*.

Brown, W. H., & Mosso, S. M. (1996, October). Inclusion in early childhood programs. Presentation at the Fifteenth Annual Conference of the South Carolina Association for the Education of Young Children (SCAEYC), Columbia, South Carolina.

Buysee, V., & Bailey, D. B. (1993). Behavioral and developmental outcomes in young children with disabilities in integrated and segregated settings: A review of comparative studies. *Journal of Special Education, 26,* 434-461.

Caldwell, B. M. (1973). The importance of beginning early. In M. B. Karnes (Ed.), *Not all wagons are red: The exceptional child's early years* (pp. 2-10). Arlington, VA: Council for Exceptional Children.

DEC Task Force on Recommended Practices. (1993). *DEC recommended practices: Indicators of quality in programs for infants and young children with special needs and their families.* Reston, VA: Council for Exceptional Children.

Guralnick, M. J. (1978). *Early intervention and the integration of handicapped and nonhandicapped children.* Baltimore: University Park Press.

Lamorey, S., & Bricker, D. D. (1993). Integrated programs: Effects on young children and their parents. In C. Peck, S. Odom, & D. Bricker (Eds.), *Integrating young children with disabilities into community-based programs: From research to implementation* (pp. 249-269). Baltimore: Paul H. Brooks.

New, R. S., & Mallory, B. L. (1994). Introduction: The ethic of inclusion. In B. L. Mallory & R. S. New (Eds.), *Diversity & developmentally appropriate practices: Challenges for early childhood education* (pp. 1-13). New York: Teachers College Press.

Odom, S. L., & McEvoy, M. A. (1988). Integration of young children with handicaps and normally developing children. In S. L.

Odom & M. B. Karnes (Eds.), *Early intervention for infants and children with handicaps: An empirical base* (pp. 241-267). Baltimore: Paul H. Brookes.

Odom, S. L., Peck, C. A., Hanson, M., Beckman, P. J., Kaiser, A. P., Lieber, J., Brown, W. H., Horn, E. M., & Schwartz, I. S. (1996). Inclusion of young children with disabilities: An ecological analysis. *Social Policy Report of the Society for Research in Child Development, 10,* 18-30.

Public Law 94-142 Education for All Handicapped Act, 1975.

Public Law 99-457 Education of the Handicapped Act Amendments, 1986.

Public Law 101-336 Americans with Disabilities Act, 1990.

Public Law 102-119 Individuals with Disabilities Education Act Amendments, 1991.

Public Law 105-17 Individuals with Disabilities Education Act Amendments, 1997.

Smith, B. J., & McKenna, P. (1994). Early intervention public policy: Past, present and future. In L. J. Johnson, R. J. Gallagher, M. J. Montagne, J. B. Jordan, J. J. Gallagher, P. L. Huntinger, & M. B. Karnes (Eds.), *Meeting early intervention challenges: Issues from birth to three* (pp. 251-264). Baltimore: Paul H. Brookes.

Trohanis, P. L. (1994). Continuing positive changes through implementation of IDEA. In L. J. Johnson, R. J. Gallagher, M. J. Montagne, J. B. Jordan, J. J. Gallagher, P. L. Huntinger, & M. B. Karnes (Eds.), *Meeting early intervention challenges: Issues from birth to three* (pp. 217-234). Baltimore: Paul H. Brookes.

United States Department of Education. (1996). *To assure the free and appropriate public education of all children with disabilities: Eighteenth Annual Report to Congress on the implementation of The Individuals with Disabilities Education Act.* Washington, DC.

Wolery, M., Strain, P. S., & Bailey, D. B. (1992). Reaching potentials of children with special needs. In S. Bredekamp & T. Rosegrant (Eds.) *Reaching potentials: Appropriate curriculum and assessment for young children* (pp. 92-111). Washington, DC: National Association for the Education of Young Children.

Wolery, M., & Wilbers, J. S. (Eds.) (1994). *Including children with special needs in early childhood programs.* Washington DC: National Association for the Education of Young Children.

Endnote

[1] Current federal law defines the least restrictive environment as "To the maximum extent appropriate, children with disabilities....are educated with children who are not disabled and special classes, separate schooling, or removal of children with disabilities from the regular environment occurs only when the nature or severity of the disability is such that education in regular classes with use of supplementary aids and services cannot be attained satisfactorily."

Table of Contents

CHAPTER 1 11
Family-Centered Practices and Inclusive Early Childhood Programs
Wesley Brown, East Tennessee State University
Center for Early Childhood Learning and Development

CHAPTER 2 27
**Collaboration and Service Coordination
in Inclusive Early Childhood Programs**
Judith A. Niemeyer and **Glenn A. Bass**
University of North Carolina, Greensboro

CHAPTER 3 49
**Activity-based Intervention Strategies for Serving Young Children
with Developmental Delays in Early Childhood Programs**
Juliann Woods Cripe and **Julia M. Lee**, Valdosta State University
Department of Special Education and Communication Disorders, Valdosta, GA

CHAPTER 4 65
**Promoting Language for Children with Developmental Delays in
Inclusive Settings: Effective Strategies for Early Childhood Educators**
Maureen A. Conroy, University of Florida, and
William H. Brown, University of South Carolina

CHAPTER 5 79
**Promoting and Supporting Peer Interactions in Inclusive Preschools:
Effective Strategies for Early Childhood Educators**
William H. Brown, University of South Carolina, and
Maureen A. Conroy, University of Florida

CHAPTER 6 109
Assistive Technology and Preschool Children: Opening Doors
Ana Lòpez-De Fede, Department of Pediatrics, and The Institute for Families in Society, and
Janice Weber, Center for Developmental Disabilities,
University of South Carolina

CHAPTER 1

Family-Centered Practices
and
Inclusive Early Childhood Programs

Wesley Brown
Center for Early Childhood Learning and Development
East Tennessee State University

"Home is the first classroom. Parents are the first and most essential teachers." (Boyer, 1991, p. 33)

Subjects & Predicates

Over the past decade, we have seen distinct movement toward two important innovations in early childhood programs, inclusive practices and family-centered practices. This book, as a whole, addresses inclusion and this chapter is organized to specifically examine the nature of family-centered practices within inclusive early childhood programs. Children's first experiences are within their families. Families are the fundamental social structure in our society and they provide the critical social context for the development of children. To examine family-centered practices, we will investigate the rationale for the family support movement and explore areas where responsive family-centered approaches to services can be provided in inclusive programs. We will discuss critical factors such as support, caring, and formal and informal networks of social support for families. How we think about families, how we communicate with them, and how we choose to serve them, can support and enhance all aspects of early childhood services for children and their families, particularly the inclusion of children with developmental delays. Family-centered practices, however, should not be reserved only for the families of children with developmental delays. Rather, family-centered services represent practices that should support and enhance the development of all children and families enrolled in early childhood programs.

Overview of Early Childhood Family-Centered Practices

Children's development is improved when parents are involved in supporting their children's learning and development. For children involved in early childhood programs, care-giving becomes a partnership between families and early childhood personnel. Significant adults in both environments are critical to achieve optimal developmental outcomes. Family-centered services represents a widely advocated approach to family support that was initially developed by the Association for the Care of Children's Health and was described as:

> ...the focus of philosophy of care in which the pivotal role of the family is recognized and respected in the lives of children with special health needs. Within this philosophy is the idea that families should be supported in their natural care-giving and decision-making roles by building on their unique strengths as people and families. In this philosophy, patterns of living at home and in the community are promoted; parents and professionals are seen as equals in a partnership committed to the development of optimal quality in the delivery of all levels of health care. To achieve this, elements of family-centered care and community-based care must be carefully interwoven into a full and effective coordination of the care of all children with special health needs (Brewer, McPherson, Magrab, & Hutchins, 1989, p. 1055).

Initially focused on children with special health care needs, the family-centered approach has been adopted by many health, education, and early childhood professionals. When examining the key elements of family-centered care developed by Shelton and Stepanek (1994) (see Table 1), one finds that they are consistent with family support principles that will be discussed later in this chapter and can be directly related to and interwoven with services provided in early childhood programs.

Family-centered principles acknowledge the central role of family members as the most knowledgeable and constant

> ## The Key Elements of Family-Centered Care
>
> - Incorporating into policy and practice the recognition that the *family is the constant* in a child's life, while the service systems and support personnel within those systems fluctuate.
> - Facilitating *family/professional collaboration* at all levels of hospital, home, and community care:
>   - care of an individual child;
>   - program development, implementation, evaluation, and evolution; and,
>   - policy formation.
> - *Exchanging complete and unbiased information* between families and professionals in a supportive manner at all times.
> - Incorporating into policy and practice the recognition *and honoring of cultural diversity,* strengths, and individuality within and across all families, *including ethnic, racial, spiritual, social, economic, educational, and geographic diversity.*
> - Recognizing and respecting *different methods of coping* and implementing comprehensive policies and programs that *provide developmental, educational, emotional, environmental, and financial supports* to meet the diverse needs of families.
> - Encouraging and facilitating *family-to-family support* and networking.
> - Ensuring that *hospital, home, and community service and support systems* for children needing specialized health and developmental care and their families are *flexible, accessible, and comprehensive* in responding to diverse family-identified needs.
> - *Appreciating families as families* and children as children, recognizing that they possess a wide range of strengths, concerns, emotions, and aspirations beyond their need for specialized health and developmental services and support.
>
> Shelton, T.L. & Stepanek, J.S. (1994). Family-centered care for children needing specialized health and developmental services. Association for the Care of Children's Health, 7910 Woodmont Avenue, Suite 300, Bethesda, Maryland 20814, 301/654-6549.
>
> **Table 1. Key Elements of Family-Centered Care**

figures in children's lives. Professionals who employ family-centered services begin working with families as they are organized, respecting and acknowledging their central and pivotal role in enhancing the development of their children. Beyond this core principle, family-centered practices address three primary areas that should receive the attention of early childhood educators. These areas briefly mentioned here are described further throughout the remainder of this chapter. The first area involves collaboration with the development of positive communication between family members and professionals. Collaboration and communication are based on parents' and professionals' mutual respect for one another and enable parent-professional partnerships to be fostered and maintained. The second area involves how we provide services. Implementing family-centered practices in early childhood programs requires shifts not only in the philosophy of how professionals think about families but in the specific practices of how we serve them. Family-centered services should be organized and delivered in a manner that makes services responsive to the needs of families. Simply providing services that professionals believe are needed is inappropriate and probably ineffective. Services must address the diversity of the families' needs rather than professionals' preconceived values and preferences for service delivery. A final critical element of family-centered practices requires that early childhood educators encourage family-to-family support. While this may represent a departure for typical early childhood programs and seem independent from their missions, it is generally very productive and often easily implemented. Family-to-family support involves employing strategies to promote connections among families. For example, many professionals have found that:

➡ providing a comfortable meeting place with contemporary information relevant to parents' needs for information;

➡ communicating parent-to-parent support activities to other families involved in your program; and

➡ supporting a volunteer parent to lead parent groups is sufficient to initiate and maintain productive parent groups. In some cases, training opportunities may be made available for parent leaders in the community (e.g., professionals' advocacy training).

Once family-to-family programs are operating, leadership can pass from parents to new parents over time. While there may be times when professionals' direct support or assistance is wanted, often these programs become self-maintaining. Frequently, one can find examples of parent support programs already in operation in many communities.

Although the concept of family-centered care originated within the health field, these principles have been incorporated within the early intervention field. The core principle of the families' pivotal role in their children's development and the three primary areas (i.e., collaboration, provision of services, and family supports) of family-centered practices will be elaborated on within the context of this chapter to provide a basis for early

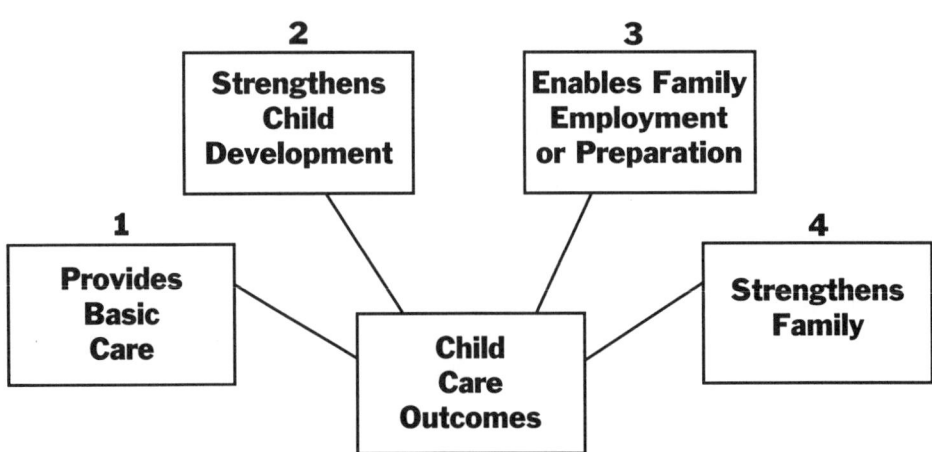

Figure 1. Family Outcomes of Caring for Children

childhood educators to implement these practices within their inclusive programs. A rationale for family involvement and recommended practices for use by early childhood educators will be discussed.

Rationale for Involvement with Families

The involvement of families in their children's child care is critical for a number of reasons. Early childhood program personnel can perform many essential roles with children as well as their families. As a result, high-quality, early childhood services may affect both the development of children and the well-being of their family members which result in a number of different outcomes including the following:

➡ provision of basic care;

➡ strengthening child development;

➡ enabling family employment; and

➡ strengthening family functioning (see Figure 1).

Providing basic care when parents cannot physically be present with their children is a primary reason parents enroll their children in early childhood programs. However, one of the wonderful outcomes of caring for children is the fact that such care can provide far more than just the basic safety and protection of children. Beyond this basic care, we know that high-quality early childhood services can strengthen children's development and their futures. The consistent stimulation and challenges provided by teachers who employ developmentally appropriate practices in early childhood programs promotes and supports children's development. Ultimately, young children become more capable and better prepared for the many tasks of late childhood and adulthood. An additional benefit of many early childhood programs is they allow parents to work or prepare for work, an important economic reality for all families. Finally, and perhaps the newest and most critical outcome area of early childhood services is "strengthening families." The concept of "strengthening families" involves enhancing the families' well-being by strengthening their ability, capacity, and capability to support their own growth and development. Strong families are better able to mobilize resources that support their needs and development. While families have long been recognized for their role in the children's development, the influence of early childhood programs in strengthening families is relatively new. The quality of the partnerships between parents and care-givers can create stability and continuity of services for children and their families. Moreover, when partnerships are not present or they are disrupted, discontinuity in children's development may occur (Berger, 1995). Particularly when families are experiencing significant changes, stable early childhood services can provide the critical support for children and their families. Optimally, children will experience continuity in care between their home and the early childhood services resulting in a number of positive outcomes for the child and family.

Supporting and Strengthening Families

Contemporary families are dynamic and ever-changing. A variety of professionals recognize the need to provide support to families and the positive outcomes of proactive support efforts. The critical role of families and their well being developed into a national movement known as the family support movement. The term family support describes various initiatives designed to support families in ways that strengthen overall family functioning and enhance the growth and development of individual family members (Dunst, Trivette, Starnes, Hamby, & Gordon, 1993; Dunst, 1995). Two major goals of family support programs include a focus on enhancing the capacity of parents in their child-rearing roles (Kagan & Weissbourd, 1994) and providing children with stable and supportive family environments (*Family Preservation and Support Services Program Act, 1993*). Through supportive programs, early childhood services can strengthen and enable families' capabilities and functioning. Dunst and his colleagues (1990; 1995) discussed six essential family support principles:

➡ enhancing a sense with community;

➡ mobilizing resources and supports;

➡ shared responsibility and collaboration;

➡ protecting family integrity;

➡ strengthening family functioning; and

➡ adopting proactive program practices.

These principles are described below in relation to early childhood settings.

Enhancing a Sense with Community

Enhancing a sense of community involves family support practices that link families and their communities together around common needs and supports. Early childhood educators can support this principle by actively linking families to other families or other community systems of support. For example, facilitating community linkages may require early childhood educators to introduce family members to other families involved in the program or to assist families in initially contacting other support or service providers in the community. Professionals may be most helpful by knowing what informal and formal community supports exist for families and then encouraging family members' use of those supports. Often, the best form of family support can be families' linkage to "informal" systems of social support. We can encourage families to reach out to other families who have had similar experiences such as having a child with a developmental delay. In some cases, well-established community resources exist that can provide families with excellent information about community services for their children within the community (e.g., The Arc: An Association for People with Mental Retardation, Downs Parents' Association, YMCA). Often, informal support may actually reduce family members' dependence on the limited resources in early childhood programs and provide them with the resources that enhance their sense of community, ultimately strengthening the family's functioning.

Mobilizing Resources and Supports

In addition to developing a sense of community, mobilizing resources and supports within the community can strengthen the family's functioning and abilities. This principle involves building support systems that are helpful to families. Again, support systems should focus on informal networks for families and

those networks could be supported by personnel in early childhood programs. For example, parents may need respite care for their child who has a developmental delay. Staff members in the early childhood center could provide parents with the names and telephone numbers of individuals and organizations that provide either informal "babysitting" services or formal respite care services. Usually these resources and sources of assistance to families are provided in their communities. Families, however, are often unaware of many potentially helpful community resources and services. Early childhood educators who become informed about community resources and who assist families in accessing them take advantage of the potential influence of community resources to enhance children's and families' well being. Often, the encouragement and assistance of a helpful early childhood educator is sufficient for family members to feel more comfortable making the initial contact with important community resources. Once the initial contact has been made, families will better understand the services, feel more comfortable with those services, and access them more readily.
Shared Responsibility and Collaboration

Sharing responsibility and collaboration is the third essential family support principle and refers to the establishment of active partnerships between parents and early childhood professionals. This principle involves mutual respect and unbiased sharing of information. Family-professional partnership is a critical factor in providing the resources and support needed by families to strengthen their functioning. Efforts by early childhood educators to encourage mutual respect and support can be most productive in building effective partnerships. Early childhood personnel can begin building partnerships by being positive models of respect and caring when working with families. When careful and respectful communication that is complete and without bias is demonstrated, professionals and families begin to build a relationship that can become a true partnership. Program personnel can build this partnership through the positive nature of their communications as described later in this chapter (see Communication and Partnership Strategies).

Protecting Family Integrity

Protecting families' integrity is a critical component for providing family support. This principle includes respect for the families' beliefs and values and protection of families from unwanted intrusions by professionals on their beliefs. Once again, collaboration is a critical component and personnel in early childhood programs should make every effort to work cooperatively with the families they serve. Often, early childhood educators have to make a special effort to accept families' beliefs and values, particularly when those values are not compatible with values held by the early childhood personnel. Although difficult, acceptance of families' values forms the basis for productive parent-professional partnership. Protecting families from professional intrusion demonstrates respect for families and sometimes requires the early childhood personnel to limit the activities they undertake, particularly those activities not desired by families. For example, consider the family that may not believe that their child needs a wheelchair to order to move around independently. Yet the staff in the early childhood program believes that a wheelchair would facilitate independence for the child. Respect of the family's belief whether it matched their own would be a way the staff could protect the family's integrity and enhance family functioning.

Strengthening Family Functioning

Strengthening family functioning involves early childhood educators employing practices that *empower* families by building on family strengths and enabling family to control decisions that are made about services for their family. Although families cannot control all aspects of early childhood programs, professionals can assist families in becoming empowered in making decisions to meet their needs within the child care center and the community. For example, personnel can encourage families to advocate for services for their children and become active participants in their children's educational decisions. Professional can encourage parents to serve on local advisory board, engage in local and state advocacy activities, and engage directly in the decision making process regarding intervention services for their child. When families are given the power to make control over their own services and the services provided to their child, they are more likely to demonstrate a greater sense of well-being, strengthening their functioning.

Adopting Proactive Program Practices.

Finally, early childhood programs can adopt proactive program practices that involve organizing early childhood services in a manner that is responsive to the desires of the families, the consumers of those services. As mentioned above, early childhood educators can include families on advisory boards and proactively request their advice about various aspects of service provision rather than making changes or including families when they express dissatisfaction with the program. Although it is not always easy to alter how we deliver services, professionals should be sensitive to families' service related needs and examine professional practices when changes are sought by many families. Fifty-nine percent of all centers involve parents in the following ways:

➡ budget preparation and programs (35%);
➡ staff selection (22%);
➡ volunteering (28%);
➡ social activities (35%); and
➡ fund raising (33%) (Powell, 1989).

Sensitive early childhood educators and responsive program practices support and strengthen families and their children and improve overall family well being. Establishing and monitoring family support is a critical component of assisting families served in early childhood programs.

In summary, supportive practices can be provided in a manner that is not intrusive for families and will ultimately strengthen their functioning. Supportive practices and parent-professional partnerships can be very rewarding for both parents and professionals. Parents and professionals should strive to establish relationships that include reasonable boundaries for both families and professionals and reflects respect for both professional judgments and family affairs. This balance referred to as a "balance theory" in the professional literature (Powell, 1989) can have positive effects on programs and their resources.

Checklist for Collaboration Between Families and Professionals

✔ How does the philosophy, policy, practice standard, or mission statement of the facility or agency reinforce that family members are essential members of the health or developmental care team?

✔ What steps are taken to ensure that families with diverse backgrounds in culture and experience are well-represented on policy, planning, advisory, and evaluation boards and committees?

✔ How are families invited and encouraged to participate in preservice and inservice training of professionals with regard to family perspectives (e.g., reimbursement for time, child care, or transportation expenses)?

✔ How are all families, regardless of cultural diversity (including ethnic, racial, spiritual, social, economic, educational, and geographic components), invited and encouraged to collaborate in the care of their child and in decision-making processes?

✔ How are families asked to define the composition of their family unit and to indicate who will be included in the collaborative process?

✔ What are the mechanisms that enable families to choose their level of participation in their children's care, and that allow families to change that level as needed or desired?

✔ How are communication and the ongoing exchange of information between and among families and professionals facilitated?

✔ How are families taught necessary skills and encouraged to participate in their children's specialized care?

✔ How is respect for the central role of families, and their expertise on their own children's reactions, temperament, strengths, and needs, facilitated and communicated?

✔ How are the opinions, concerns, and priorities of family members recognized as essential information and incorporated into all care planning and decision making?

✔ Are meetings/visits scheduled at times convenient for families, and are the agenda items developed collaboratively between families and professionals?

✔ What are the mechanisms that ensure families access to their children's medical records, and how is family input incorporated into medical records?

Shelton, T.L. & Stepanek, J.S. (1994). Family-centered care for children need in a specialized health and developmental services. Association for the Care of Children's Health, 7910 Woodmont Avenue, Suite 300, Bethesda, Maryland 20814, 301/654-6549.

Table 2. Checklist for Collaboration

Recommended Practices for Providing Family-Centered Practices

What are the major challenges to becoming more family-centered? Expanding our philosophical concept of early childhood education to actively include families is the initial step to becoming more family-centered. Fostering parents to become more than a secondary audience for early childhood services is another critical step. Forming effective partnerships with families and finding ways to include, support, and empower families within the constraints of early childhood service systems is also critical. Professionals should be concerned about the quality of their relationships and communications with families. Developing broader conceptions of community, the relationship of community to early childhood programs, and ways to help link families to the community and its natural supports requires substantial change for personnel working in many early childhood programs. Becoming a "family-friendly" service system that is flexible in service delivery and that focuses on families' strengths and the enhancement of the families' unit, whatever the families' cultural context or configuration requires a shift in thinking about early childhood practices.

Shifts in how we think about serving children and families will not come easily given the historical nature of early childhood services (i.e., primary interest and focus on children) and the economic constraints within our society. However, once implemented, the benefits derived from family-centered services will encourage early childhood educators to continue to use the principles of family-centered practices. To the extent that we can focus on multiple generations, children and their families, we will find improvement in families' well-being through the implementation of these services.

Collaboration with Families

As discussed previously, collaboration is an initial, critical component for implementation of family-centered services. What are our recommended practices for collaboration? Several prerequisite skills for early childhood educators include:

➡ acceptance of and respect for families;

➡ good communication and problem-solving skills;

➡ a willingness to completely share information;

➡ a willingness to establish and maintain mutually beneficial partnerships with families; and

➡ develop and implementation of procedures to link families with resources within their communities.

In many cases, these prerequisites will require a shift in what professionals believe and how we deliver services. Nevertheless, early childhood educators can begin with a positive perspective when thinking about and working collaboratively with parents and family members. Often, families can solve problems with positive support from early childhood professionals. Program directors need to recruit personnel who resemble and identify with the families served by the program. For example, hiring professionals who can accept and respect the families' values and decisions, even when they do not represent what they believe or think, can be critical. Professionals' familiarity with family-centered principles will allow families to make choices and define their levels of involvement in the program. One result of collaboration is that parents feel welcome to observe, participate, and discuss program policies and practices.

Table 2 contains an excellent checklist for agency personnel to evaluate collaboration between families and professionals. The checklist developed by Shelton and Stepanek (1994) contains twelve questions that allow early childhood educators to examine numerous features in their own program and explore how those features respond to, involve, and provide for family-centered practices. Often, nonprofit programs are flexible and organized to allow personnel to address the questions on the checklist. However, all early childhood educators are encouraged to examine their collaborative efforts and to seek innovative strategies to improve collaboration between families and professionals. For example, early childhood personnel might ask several staff members to meet and review the questions on the checklist and to examine the current status of their program. Following this assessment, personnel might plan strategies that would allow them to implement collaborative practices within their programs.

The involvement of families and professional acceptance of family choices supports early childhood educators' efforts to improve children's development. Professionals who build family strengths and empower families to mobilize resources maximize families' influence on their children's development. Are we able to accept new collaborative roles and take the initiative to actively involve families? Are we personally invested in family-centered and inclusive practices for children with developmental delays? Are we philosophically compatible with collaborative practices? These are questions early childhood program staff should consider.

Communication and Partnership Strategies with Families

Communication and partnerships between families and professionals are critical strategies to enhance parent-professional collaboration and family-centered services. How well do we communicate with families? Good parent-professional communication is essential to achieve our partnerships with families. Positive communication and agreed upon expectations between families and professionals form the basis for understanding and mutual support, rather than misunderstanding and competition. Most important to building a partnership with families is establishing a solid relationship with them. Excellent relationships can be established and based upon the positive interactions parents and professionals have developed while serving young children. Effective communication requires careful listening and responding to family members' concerns and priorities. Working directly with family members to develop alternative ways to solve family-determined problems can result in strengthened collaborative relationships. An effective working relationship can strengthen family functioning and, ultimately, reduce many difficulties associated with children's and families' participation in early childhood programs.

As discussed earlier, reaching out to families can be mutually beneficial and early childhood educators who employ partnership as one of their program out-

> **Recommended Readings**
>
> Bishop, K. K., Woll, J., & Arango, P. (1993). Family/professional collaboration for children with special health care needs and their families. Burlington, VT: Family/Professional Collaboration Project.
>
> Bronfenbrenner, U. (1979). Ecology of the family as a context for human development. Developmental Psychology, 22, 723-742.
>
> Family Resource Coalition. (1996). Guidelines for family support practice. Chicago, IL: Family Resource Coalition.
>
> Jeppson, E. S., & Thomas, J. (1995). Essential allies: Families as advisors. Bethesda, MD: Institute for Family-Centered Care.
>
> Johnson, B. H., Jeppson, E. S., & Redburn, L. (1992). Caring for children and their families: Guidelines for hospitals. Bethesda, MD: The Association for the Care of Children's Health.
>
> Kraemer, J. (1993). Building villages to raise our children: Collaboration. Massachusetts: Harvard Family Research Project.
>
> Larner, M. (1995). Linking family support and early childhood programs: Issues, experiences, opportunities. Chicago: Family Research Coalition.
>
> Weiss, H. B., Woodburn, A., Lopez, M.E., & Kramer, J. (1993). Building villages to raise our children: From programs to service systems. Massachusetts: Harvard Family Research Project.
>
> Wolery, M., Strain, P.S., & Bailey, D.B. (1992). Reaching potential of children with special needs. In S. Bredekamp, & T. Rosegrant (Eds.), Reaching potential: Appropriate curriculum and assessment for young children. Washington, DC: National Association for the Education of the Young.
>
> **Table 3.**

comes promote the strengthening of families. Partnerships can lead to a greater investment by parents in their child's development and early childhood services. Enhanced communications and support between families and professionals will reduce stress and frustration for both families and early childhood professionals. Early childhood personnel can become family-centered professionals and strengthen their relationships with families. Unfortunately, there will never be enough professional services to meet all families' needs. However, we can shift both our philosophy and nature of services to become more family-centered and more successful for families, including those families with children who have developmental delays.

Beckman (1996) discussed nine areas of professional practice that influence communication skills and enable providers to be more effective in their partnerships with families:

- *How providers listen to families* is a critical element for professionals who work with families. Staff training that focuses on enhancing listening skills should assist early childhood personnel in becoming better listeners when working with families.

- *Respect for families* is also fundamental for the development of effective partnerships. Again, staff development activities that enable early childhood educators to understand and value families with cultural and socioeconomic differences might assist personnel in acquiring more positive attitudes about families.

- *How providers characterize families* represents another practice which influences how early childhood educators work with families. If the family characterizations by personnel do not reflect true acceptance and respect, distance between the professionals and families will prevent optimal development for the children.

- *Professionals' sensitivity* also is essential to developing relationships with families as well. Again, staff development can promote sensitivity to family issues and needs (e.g., sensitivity to the emotional support needs or financial concerns a family may have). Such sensitivity becomes a foundation for further communication and collaboration.

- *The way service is obtained,* another important practice, is influenced by the resources and design of the service system. Nevertheless, resourceful professionals can influence how families receive services from early childhood programs.

- *How meetings are conducted* is a reflection of early childhood educators' attitudes about working with families. How initial meetings are conducted and the nature of parent-professional communication allows family members to begin their partnership with early childhood educators.

- *The way multiple professionals interact* reflects on staff-to-staff interactions about families and can support or distress families who are attempting to deal with the special needs of their children (i.e., if there is positive communication among staff members then families may be more comfortable).

- *How programs are structured* reflects how programs are designed to be able to serve families as well as reflects professional practices implemented in these programs.

- *How differences are resolved* when families and professionals have disagreements.

Once again, examining communication skills and the content of communication, along with, methods of working with families to resolve conflicts and form a partnership is essential in resolving disagreements. Table three includes references for further reading on family support and family-centered practices. These resources may be of assistance with developing family-centered approaches in early childhood programs. As outlined in all of these principles, *how* early childhood professionals view and include families in services are critical components for fostering communication and the development of partnerships.

Special Supports for Children with Developmental Delays

Young children who have developmental delays may be involved with services from many agencies or programs. Two federal programs from IDEA, the Individuals with Disabilities Education Act, serve children from birth to age three and from three through five years of age. Regulations for these programs require early childhood services in natural or least restrictive settings and inclusive early childhood programs. When early childhood programs are selected as environments for early intervention services, the children and families should have a service coordinator who assists the family in obtaining and monitoring children's services. Service coordinators should be knowledgeable about young children with developmental delays, available resources, and requirements relative to early intervention. They should assist families in dealing with children's service providers. When a service coordinator is available for families, early childhood educators should not need to spend much time assisting the family with linkages to external resources and can focus more on relationship building with families. However, researchers have also noted that personnel in early childhood programs often provide some level of service coordination to children and families (Powell, 1989). The National Day Care Study collected information at more than three thousand early childhood centers and found that 90% of centers provided some of the following services: family counseling on child development; general family counseling; assistance with obtaining foods stamps or financial aid; and assistance with obtaining other community services (Powell, 1989). Most early childhood programs provided family counseling related to child development, one third of the centers studied reported providing all of the above services, and only ten percent of centers reported providing none of the services. Although not all early childhood programs provided these services, they may be available for some families who identify them as needs.

If the early childhood program is selected as an inclusive early intervention site, other forms of services or assistance may be available to personnel working in the program and to the families served. These services or supports may include special materials and equipment required for an individual child (e.g., adaptive seating, assistive technology) that compensate for sensory or physical difficulties. An early interventionist may be assigned to provide consultation with early childhood educators and may visit the early childhood program to provide special instruction. In addition, related service personnel such as speech and language therapists, physical therapists, or occupational therapists may visit the early childhood center to provide consultation or one-to-one therapy. Transportation to and from the early childhood center may also be provided for children with developmental delays. Occasionally children will first attend a special program and then be transported to an early childhood program rather than home, with the early childhood service being either an early intervention service or strictly an early childhood program selected by the family to meet their child care needs.

Conclusion

The application of family-centered practices and the general practices of family support have enabled early childhood programs to achieve more meaningful relationships with the families they serve. Effective parent-professional partnerships may further enhance children's and families' development. These positive outcomes have benefited families, children, and early childhood educators. Collaboratively and collectively, families and early childhood professionals can accomplish far more than they might independently. When programs implement family support practices, they enable families to benefit from a broader array of community resources and services and begin to develop and support families' own capacities for finding resources and benefiting from informal systems of support. These practices benefit all children attending the early childhood programs and support inclusive services for children with developmental delays.

References

Beckman, P. J. (Ed.). (1996). *Strategies for working with families of young children with disabilities.* Baltimore: Paul H. Brookes.

Berger, E. H. (1995). *Parents as partners in education: Families and schools working together.* Englewood Cliffs, NJ: Merrill.

Boyer, E. L. (1991). *Ready to learn: A mandate for the nation.* Princeton: The Carnegie Foundation for the Advancement of Teaching.

Brewer, E. J., McPherson, M., Magrab, P. R., & Hutchins, V. L. (1989). Family-centered, community-based, coordinated care for children with special health care needs. *Pediatrics, 83,* 1055-1060.

Dunst, C. J. (1990). Family support principles: Checklists for program builders and practitioners. *Family Systems Intervention Monograph 2* (5). Morganton, NC: Family, Infant and Preschool Program, Western Carolina Center.

Dunst, C. J. (1995). *Key characteristics and features of community-based family support programs.* Chicago: Family Resource Coalition.

Dunst, C. J., Trivette, C. M., Starnes, A. L., Hamby, D. W., & Gordon, N. J. (1993). *Building and evaluating family support initiatives.* Baltimore: Paul H. Brookes.

Family Preservation and Support Services Program Act (1993). Public Law 103-166. Washington, DC: United States Congress.

Kagan, S. L., & Weissbourd, B. (Eds.). (1994). *Putting families first: America's family support movement and the challenge of change.* San Francisco: Jossey-Bass Publishers.

Powell, D. R. (1989). *Families and early childhood programs.* Washington: National Association for the Education of Young Children.

Shelton, T. L., & Stepanek, J. S. (1994). *Family-centered care for children needing specialized health and developmental services* (Third Edition). Bethesda, MD: Association for the Care of Children's Health.

CHAPTER 2

Collaboration and Service Coordination in Inclusive Early Childhood Programs

Judith A. Niemeyer
and
Glenn A. Bass
University of North Carolina, Greensboro

> *"The process of service coordination should include collaboration between family members and any service providers involved with providing services to children with developmental delays and their families."*

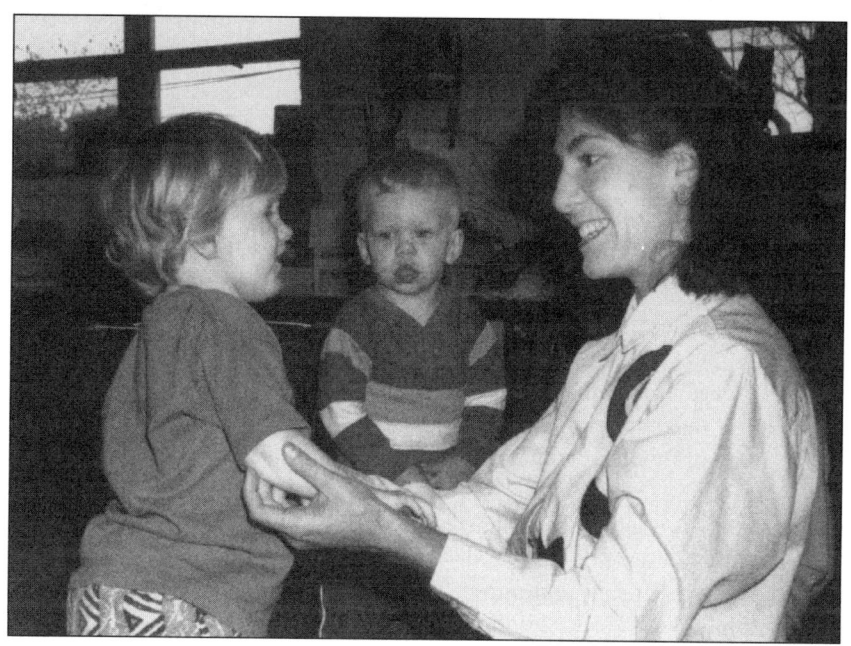

In recent years many young children with developmental delays have received early childhood special education services in community programs that serve young children without developmental delays (e.g., child care programs, preschools, Head Start Programs). Frequently, children with developmental delays have received services related to their developmental needs from professionals and paraprofessionals working in different agencies and in a variety of settings (e.g., health care programs, speech and hearing clinics, homes). For example, it is not uncommon for a three-year-old child with cerebral palsy who is enrolled in an inclusive early childhood program to receive speech therapy, physical therapy, occupational therapy, and itinerant early childhood special education services while enrolled in a community child care center. Related services such as speech therapy and physical therapy services may be implemented at home and provided by personnel working for a private agency. In addition, the child may require ongoing medical monitoring by a neurologist, pediatrician, dentist, and other health related personnel. Often, a child's family has much of the responsibility for coordinating and monitoring necessary services.

Whereas the birth and care of children with developmental delays may be difficult for many families, the coordination of the services provided by different agencies can be overwhelming at times. Given the variety of services children with developmental delays require, early childhood professionals should become partners with families in the service coordination process for securing appropriate assistance in inclusive early childhood programs. In this chapter we will discuss:

➡ a rationale for service coordination and the importance of collaboration;

➡ several models of collaboration;

➡ the benefits and challenges of collaboration and service coordination; and

➡ strategies for building collaborative partnerships.

Rationale for Service Coordination and Collaboration

The involvement of families in early childhood programs has a long-standing history in early childhood education (Bailey, 1994; Swick, 1993). Historically, service coordination has been viewed as a systematic process for assisting parents and family members in obtaining any services and resources they need (Weil & Karls, 1989). Because services and resources for young children with developmental delays and their families have been fragmented across different personnel, agencies, and settings, professionals have recognized a critical need for better coordination of services (Bailey, 1994). The primary purpose of service coordination has been to promote the timely procurement of services and resources for children and their families. Service coordination often includes providing information about services and resources available to children and their families, and when indicated, promoting linkages to those services and resources. Specifically, service coordination includes coordinating:

➡ evaluations and assessments;

➡ delivery of early intervention services;

➡ health providers services; and

➡ development and monitoring of each

child's individual program plan [i.e., Individualized Educational Plans (IEPs), Individualized Family Service Plans (IFSPs)]. In addition, service coordination also helps family members identify supportive community resources such as advocacy services and parent-to-parent networks.

The rationale for service coordination and collaboration is relatively straightforward and twofold. First, because of the critical nature of service coordination and collaboration, federal legislation has been directed at enhancing service coordination and collaboration among professionals and families of young children with developmental delays. Several federal initiatives were developed to:

➡ promote the development of young children with developmental delays and minimize future developmental risks;

➡ reduce the educational costs for schools;

➡ maximize the potential independence of individuals with developmental delays; and

➡ enable families to care for their child with developmental delays [*Public Law 94-142 (1975)*; *Public Law 99-457 (1986)*; *Public Law 101-576 (1990)*; *Public Law 102-119 (1991)*; *Public Law 105-17 (1997)*].

Indeed, with infants and toddlers with developmental delays and their families, service coordination has been required as a specific component of their Individualized Family Service Plans (IFSPs) (e.g., *Public Law 99-457*).

Second, in recent years, service coordination and collaboration have become recommended practice in early childhood special education (DEC Task Force on Recommended Practices, 1993; Odom & McLean, 1996). Because young children with developmental delays have complex needs and many service providers are involved with their families, no single profession or agency has all of the knowledge and expertise needed to meet children's and families' needs (Bruder & Bologna, 1993). Therefore, service providers and families should collaborate and use their collective resources and expertises to provide effective services for children and their families without unnecessary duplication of services. To facilitate collaboration and coordination of services, local communities are encouraged to develop formal and informal interagency agreements to ensure the timely delivery of services and resources. Further detail on interagency agreements and interagency collaboration will be discussed later in the section on collaborative models.

The process of service coordination should include collaboration between family members and any service providers involved with providing services to children with developmental delays and their families. Effective service coordination should result in family members' direct involvement in determining which services and resources will be accessed and used. During the past decade, a shift from "child-centered" service provision (i.e., viewing the child as the focus of services) to "family-centered" intervention (i.e., viewing the family as the focus of services) has transpired in early childhood special education. The transition from child-focused to family-focused service provision has changed professionals' responsibilities from being "experts and primary decision makers" to supportive roles of "collaborators" with family members (Shelton & Stepanek, 1994; Winton, 1986).

Directly involving families in making decisions about their lives in general and their children in particular should result in better parent-professional collaboration. In addition, enhanced collaboration between families and professionals should result in improved implementation of mutually agreed upon goals for children and their families. For example, if professionals pressure a family to take their child with a motor disability to physical therapy services that are inconveniently located and at times difficult for family members, parents may not follow through on therapy visits or may attend therapy sessions only sporadically. Although professionals may have the child's developmental interests in mind by recommending a goal of regular physical therapy (i.e., a "professionally driven" goal), they may not have been sensitive and responsive to the very realistic concerns affecting the family (e.g., resources needed to travel to therapy, lack of transportation, competing family priorities). Through collaborative planning, however, professionals and family members may plan for the "best possible solution" for arranging regular physical therapy services. For example, for families with limited resources (e.g., lack of reliable transportation) or competing priorities (e.g., both parents employed), home-based therapy services or itinerant therapy at the child care center may be the best option for promoting regular therapy sessions. Based on a family-centered philosophy, Leviton, Mueller, and Kauffman (1992) argued that family members are the ultimate decision makers and professionals should be supportive consultants by assisting families in making decisions and solving potential problems. With close collaboration with family members, services and resources will be based on individual families' concerns, priorities, and resources.

Although the shift from child-centered to family-centered services has been supported by many early childhood professionals, it also may pose concerns for professionals. Philosophically, adoption of family-centered practices requires that family members become active decision makers and be included in all aspects of their children's programs (Bailey, Simeonsson, Yoder, & Huntington, 1990). Family-centered intervention and service coordination are radical shifts from traditional "expert" models of practice when professionals merely informed families of education and intervention decisions (Turnbull & Turnbull, 1990). By directly involving family members in service coordination, empowerment of family members becomes an important dimension of service coordination that may enable families to procure their own services and resources in the future (Dunst & Trivette, 1989; Dunst, Trivette, & Deal, 1994). When families become empowered, they become more competent and capable and can better meet their families' needs. Inherent in contemporary empowerment approaches is establishing and nurturing collaborative relationships between family members and professionals involved in service provision.

If on the other hand, professionals assume their traditional roles and attempt to make decisions about services and resources, family members will be removed from the service coordination process. This may create a situation where family members become overly dependent on the professionals or they may not follow through on recommendations that were developed without their direct participation in the planning process. Although inadvertent, removing family members from the service coordination process may inhibit their ability to be or become independent decision-makers with respect to their children's and families' needs. Therefore, it is important for professionals to work in both a supportive and educative manner with family members to help them acquire and better understand critical information about services and resources that might be beneficial to their children and families. In addition, family members should be supported in becoming proactive decision-makers who collaborate with professionals about which services and resources should be employed to meet their families' needs.

In summary, in recent years service coordination and collaboration have become a critical service delivery components for providing high-quality services to young children with developmental delays and their families. Although contemporary methods of service coordination should vary based on the needs of children and the preferences of their parents, the goal of any service coordination process should be for professionals to work collaboratively with family members. This is accomplished by providing information about community services and resources and then by assisting and supporting family members while they access those services and resources (Bailey, 1994). For further detail on collaboration with families see Chapter 1 of this book (W. Brown, 1997).

Models of Collaboration

As discussed above, effective service coordination for young children with developmental delays involves active collaboration among professionals and families. Collaboration can be defined as "cooperation among two or more people (or agencies) concerning a particular undertaking" (Dunst & Paget, 1991, p. 27). Some professionals view collaboration as a partnership but it also implies a relationship that evolves over time between two or more individuals. When examining the service coordination process for young children with developmental delays, several types of collaboration may be involved:

➡ collaboration among families and professionals;

➡ collaboration among professionals; and

➡ collaboration among different agencies. These forms of collaboration will be discussed individually, however, one should be careful to remember that they are all interrelated and necessary for effective and efficient service coordination and collaboration.

Collaboration Among Families and Professionals

In early childhood programs, collaboration among families and professionals is critical. Because families play a primary role in providing and securing services and resources for their young children with developmental delays, they should be directly involved in the planning and intervention process from initial assessment to subsequent program development and implementation and, finally, to evaluation of individualized plans. A collaborative relationship among the family members and professionals is often conceptualized as a partnership. Dunst and Paget (1991) suggested four characteristics of family-professional partnerships. First, all members of partnerships contribute in some meaningful way to family-professional relationships (e.g., critical information, their cumulative expertise). Second, all participants voluntarily enter into family-professional relationships. Third, honesty and trust form the basis of partnerships and all relevant information should be shared completely by members of partnerships. Fourth, all decisions are made by individuals designated by members of the partnership. As recommended earlier, parents should make decisions related to services and resources and professionals should serve as collaborative consultants to family members.

Family-centered practice is a contemporary model for collaboration among families and professionals and the model requires that family members be active participants in planning, implementing, and evaluating the individualized plans of children (i.e., IEPs) and families (i.e., IFSPs). Families can collaborate with professionals in multiple ways. First, family members should play a key role in any assessment process. Linder (1993) recommended a collaborative partnership with families during the assessment process from the initial referral to the actual assessment. In almost all cases, parents know their children much better than professionals and they have a wealth of information to contribute toward completion of any comprehensive assessment. When parents are actively involved in assessment and intervention plans, they become partners, and their relationships with professionals become more collaborative. Indeed, the assessment process is usually the first step in the establishment of a positive and mutually beneficial family-professional relationship.

Second, family members and professionals can collaborate during service provision. When family members are involved in the assessment and planning process, they become active "stakeholders" and more likely to implement collaboratively determined goals for their children and families. Therefore, parents become significant partners in the development of individual programs for their children and families [i.e., Individualized Family Service Plans (IFSPs)] and children [Individualized Education Plans (IEPs)]. Third, many family members may choose to become directly involved in developmentally enhancing activities with their children. For example, they may implement physical therapy exercises at home to build and maintain motor strength and language interventions at home as well as in community settings to augment school-based interventions which further support children's language development.

Family members' active involvement in assessment, planning, and implementation of collaboratively determined goals should promote and support the emergence of family-professional partnerships. For example, Bloch and Seitz (1989) developed a "family friendly" assessment that facilitates the development of collaboration and partnerships among parents and professionals. Using the Bloch and Seitz approach, both parents and professionals complete a developmental checklist based on their observations of children in their homes and classrooms. The assessment results are discussed in a meeting in which the parents and professionals are members of collaborative teams, and intervention strategies are planned based on collaborative assessment information. A collaborative assessment and planning process may promote parents' feelings of competency as well as their feelings of being significant participants on their children's planning team.

Several programmatic examples of family-professional partnerships have been developed in recent years including:
- The Family, Infant, and Preschool Program (FIPP)
- Child Development Resources (CDR)
- Project BLEND.

The Family, Infant, and Preschool Program (FIPP) in Morganton, North Carolina, is an example of a rural program whose personnel have implemented family-centered practices for a number of years (for description see McGonigel & Garland, 1988). FIPP personnel actively involve children's parents in the assessment process and the development of all intervention strategies. Parents identify the needs of their children and families by completing "family friendly" assessments of children's and families' needs and priorities. Family members also participate in follow-up interviews with a professional team member. Following an initial assessment process, family members and professionals collaboratively develop an outline of the intervention plans and identify each team member's role and responsibilities for implementing specific parts of the plan (i.e., an action plan).

Personnel in another early intervention program, Child Development Resources (CDR) in Lightfoot, Virginia, also practice family-centered principles (for description see McGonigel & Garland, 1988). Similar to FIPP, program personnel work collaboratively with parents to determine families' needs while serving as collaborative consultants to assist families in achieving their priorities for accessing community services and resources. Professionals work closely with family members in determining their families' needs and identifying community service and resource options. During the planning and intervention process, parents make all final decisions about the services and resources that will be provided to their families.

A final example of parent-professional partnership has been Project BLEND, a model demonstration program in Nashville, Tennessee, whose staff members have provided early intervention services to families with young children with developmental delays (Brown, Horn, Heiser, & Odom, in press). Similar to both the FIPP and CDR programs, Project BLEND evolved into an indirect service delivery model that emphasized the development of parent-professional partnerships to support young children's inclusion in community-based child care programs. Itinerant early childhood special educators worked collaboratively with family members, child care personnel, and related service personnel (e.g., speech therapist, physical therapist) to insure that collaborative teams were established with parents as active team members in planning services for their children. The primary role of BLEND personnel was to promote team communication and collaboration while coordinating service and resource procurement with families. Personnel in the three early intervention programs discussed above, as well as professionals in many other programs across the nation, have demonstrated that with family-professional collaboration, professionals can be more sensitive and responsive to family members' concerns and priorities for services for their children and families.

Collaboration Among Professionals

Service providers working in inclusive early childhood programs may include early childhood teachers, early childhood special educators, paraprofessionals, and various related services personnel (e.g., occupational therapists, physical therapists, speech therapists, nurses). Collaboration among service providers from various disciplines is critical for inclusion of young children with developmental delays in early childhood programs. A contemporary collaborative approach that is used often in inclusive early childhood settings is a transdisciplinary team approach (Raver, 1991; Rainforth, York, & MacDonald, 1992). A transdisciplinary team is defined as a collaborative team of professionals, paraprofessionals, and parents who share information, knowledge, and professional skills to plan and implement individualized programs for children with developmental delays. The sharing of expertise across traditional disciplinary boundaries is a critical aspect of transdisciplinary teams (Eagen, Petisi, & Toole, 1980; Orelove & Sobsey, 1987).

Using a transdisciplinary approach, various early childhood professionals, irrespective of their specific discipline, work together with family members as a collaborative team to promote the common interest of children with developmental delays. Several common characteristics appear to support the success of a transdisciplinary approach. First, team members from different disciplines must recognize that no single discipline has a monopoly on the expertise needed to provide effective early childhood services to children with developmental delays and their families. Hence, mutual respect and value of the contributions of other team members and disciplines is a necessary condition for effective collaborative teaming. Second, team members must be willing to share their expertise and work toward implementing and evaluating different intervention strategies on behalf of children with developmental delays and their families. Finally, team members must have similar and mutually agreed upon goals for children with developmental delays.

For example, a young child with oral motor disabilities that affect eating and talking is often served by a number of highly specialized professionals (e.g., occupational therapists, speech and language pathologists). Professionals involved with the child and the child's parents might establish a transdisciplinary team to review relevant assessment information and to plan practical intervention strategies. During collaborative team planning, an occupational therapist and speech therapist might suggest various intervention procedures and preschool teachers and parents would discuss the feasibility of implementing those strategies within routine classroom and home activities. As a transdisciplinary team and through consensus, team members will determine which intervention strategies will be used to promote the child's oral motor abilities. Usually, team members who have direct and frequent contact with the child are selected (e.g., teachers, parents) to implement any mutually agreed upon interventions within preschool activities. In the case of a child with oral motor difficulties, an occupational therapist, speech therapist, teacher, paraprofessional, and parent work closely as team members to implement and evaluate oral motor development interventions (e.g., eating thickly textured foods during meals, sucking liquids through a straw, having the child imitate difficult to pronounce sounds and words) within common activities in the child's preschool program and at home.

Once transdisciplinary team members decide on a course of action, members with the most relevant expertise can provide collaborative consultation and technical assistance to the team members who implement interventions within inclusive preschool classrooms. Typical forms of collaborative consultation and technical assistance include observing adults who implement intervention strategies and, when needed, providing constructive feedback on how to improve implementation of interventions. In addition, during collaborative consultation, consultants can actually demonstrate effective intervention strategies to adults who work regularly with children with developmental delays during common preschool activities and circumstances. The primary objective of sharing their professional expertise with direct service personnel and parents is to increase the number of teaching and learning opportunities for children with developmental delays during common preschool activities. The ongoing technical assistance provided by transdisciplinary team members may promote effective implementation and evaluation of children's individualized interventions. Similar to partnerships with parents, partnerships among professionals are based on planning and implementing practical plans with regular and frequent communication about how children's individualized plans are working and, when indicated, how they can be improved.

The collaborative relationships between early childhood educators and early childhood special educators are similar to the partnerships established with transdisciplinary teams. Two common models of early childhood and early childhood special education collaboration exist: a team teaching model and a collaborative consultation model. With both models, early childhood educators and early childhood special educators function as a collaborative team working together to provide appropriate early childhood services for young children with developmental delays and their families.

In a team teaching model, the early childhood education teacher and the early childhood special education teacher work together in the same preschool setting with children with and without developmental delays, and they collaborate on planning, organization, and implementation of educational programs for all children in their classroom. Both teachers are partners in their classroom and have equal professional responsibilities. Often, they compliment one another by bringing different professional training and expertise to the implementation of early childhood services. For example, an early childhood educator may have extensive knowledge of child development and may know how to motivate and involve young children in developmentally appropriate activities. The early childhood special educator may have extensive knowledge of how to identify the individual needs of children with developmental delays, how to adapt the classroom activities to meet any identified needs, how to implement appropriate strategies for socially including young children with developmental delays in a variety of preschool activities, and how to develop intervention strategies to promote specific developmental competencies (e.g., activity-based interventions, peer-initiated social skills interventions). Similar to a transdisciplinary team although on a smaller scale, team teachers work collaboratively with both sharing their knowledge and professional expertise about young children. Although team teaching often presents professional challenges to teachers, the benefits of co-teaching with collaborative planning should provide better inclusive services for young children with and without developmental delays. In addition, across time as co-teachers establish effective working partnerships, a natural exchange of their complementary expertise should occur and improve the professional competencies of both early childhood and early childhood special educators.

With another model, a collaborative consultation model, early childhood special educators indirectly serve a number of children with developmental delays and are usually accountable for supporting the planning, implementing, and evaluating of those children's individualized plans. With this model, children with developmental delays are served in a number of preschool settings throughout the community. In a collaborative consultation model, early childhood special educators are responsible for the cooperative development of the Individualized Education Plans (IEPs) or the Individualized Family Service Plans (IFSPs) and on-going professional support and consultation on the implementation of strategies for achieving children's individualized goals. Their responsibility often includes monitoring children's progress toward goal attainment and completion of paperwork for individualized plans. In this model, early childhood educators are responsible for all children in the classroom including the children with developmental delays. Similar to team members on a transdisciplinary team, early childhood special educators work collaboratively with early childhood educators and provide collaborative consultation and technical assistance on specific intervention strategies to implement for children with developmental delays during activities in early childhood classrooms. Using this model, early childhood special educators visit children's classrooms regularly (e.g., weekly, every other week), and they observe and work with children during common classroom activities. By working with children with and without developmental delays during normal classroom conditions, itinerant early childhood special educators develop a better understanding of what interventions and activities are feasible, given the resources and circumstances of children's classroom teachers. In addition, they are able to monitor the developmental progress of children with developmental delays within inclusive programs. In support of the inclusion of young children with developmental delays, itinerant early childhood special educators may serve a number of important functions. For example, they may provide important information to the early childhood educator about:

➡ critical characteristics of specific disabilities;

➡ how to adapt materials and routine activities to promote and support children with developmental delays active engagement in classroom activities; and

➡ how to develop and implement feasible technical assistance plans (e.g., relevant inservices, informal sharing of important information, effective use of highly specialized consultants). This information is typically based on the early childhood educators self-identified needs (Wesley, 1994).

Within a collaborative consultation model, early childhood special educators are responsible for collaborative development and monitoring of individualized plans, and early childhood education teachers are the primary implementers of those plans within an inclusive classroom. Because of the critical role of early childhood educators, they should attend planning meetings and be involved integrally in the collaborative development of any individualized plans. As the educator who has the most contact with children with and without developmental delays and the team member with the most knowledge about their classroom, early childhood educators should share important information about children's current abilities and successes in preschool activities with itinerant early childhood special educators. Most important, early childhood education teachers, in consultation with early childhood special educators, will be responsible for implementing classroom interventions that are related to children's goals from their individualized plans. Hence, an effective partnership can ensure the practicality of individualized plans and provide an important professional support system for planning and implementing plans for children with developmental delays within inclusive early childhood settings.

In summary, collaboration among service providers who work with young children with developmental delays is critical to providing inclusive early childhood services. Although collaborative strategies may differ in the number of people involved and where intervention will be provided, two common elements appear to be important. First, an understanding that multiple professionals can and should contribute to individual planning and implementation of services is critical for serving young children with developmental delays and their families. Second, adoption of effective strategies that allow professionals and parents to organize assessment information and collaboratively plan interventions across significant people and settings is important for effective implementation of children's individualized plans. When service providers work cooperatively in the "best interest" of children with developmental delays and their families, the professional challenges that are inherent in service provision for young children with developmental difficulties can be addressed within inclusive early childhood programs.

Collaboration Among Agencies

Similar to family-professional and professional-professional collaboration, collaboration among community and state agencies is important for the effective delivery of services to young children with developmental delays. As mentioned earlier, the multiple needs of young children with developmental delays and their families require the involvement of professionals from a variety of disciplines and those professionals may work in a number of local programs and state agencies. Agencies and programs that may be involved in the delivery of services or supports to young children with developmental delays and their families include:

➡ social services (e.g., public assistance programs, child abuse programs);

➡ health services (e.g., public health nursing, home health services);

➡ educational services (e.g., early childhood special education programs, assistive technology centers, diagnostic and evaluation centers);

➡ public and private medical services (e.g., pediatricians, neurologists, psychologists, physical therapy); and

➡ advocacy services (e.g., family support groups, parent-to-parent programs).

Typically, collaboration among state agencies is formalized with written agreements outlining the roles and responsibilities for personnel in the participating agencies. Personnel in local agencies, however, often collaborate with one another informally in a number of important areas including:

➡ child identification and referral activities;

➡ service coordination and service provision;

➡ collaborative training activities;

➡ financial arrangements to promote timely service delivery and reimbursement;

➡ child and family advocacy; and

➡ public policy development.

Interagency collaboration on the state level has been required by in federal legislation [e.g., *Public Law 99-457 (1986)*, *Public Law 102-119 (1991) Public Law 105-17 (1997)*]. Federal legislation has mandated that State Interagency Coordinating Councils (ICCs) be established and maintained in each state to provide guidance to state agencies in developing policies and procedures and to coordinate preservice and inservice training (Bruder & Bologna, 1993). Membership on the State Interagency Coordinating Councils is specified in federal legislation and consists of family members, state agency representatives, direct service providers, and Institutions of Higher Education training personnel. The governance structure of the State Interagency Coordinating Councils and its working subgroups varies from state to state.

An example of interagency collaboration on the state level is in the area of personnel preparation in North Carolina. Inservice training activities are developed collaboratively by critical personnel in several state agencies, and funding for training activities is provided by those agencies. With state level interagency collaboration, early childhood personnel across the state have better access to high-quality training opportunities (North Carolina State Interagency Coordinating Council, 1994). For example, in North Carolina, regional teams of professionals and parents plan training activities for personnel working with young children with and without developmental delays. Regional teams are comprised of professionals from critical state agencies (e.g., Division of Public Instruction, Division of Maternal and Child Health, Department of Human Resources), family members, teacher trainers from Institutions of Higher Education (e.g., university and community college faculty members), and direct service personnel (e.g., teachers, early interventionists), with funds and resources being provided by participating state agencies. Inservice topics have included:

➡ Understanding the Local and Statewide Early Intervention System;

➡ Working Effectively with Families;

➡ Recommended Curriculum Practices; and

➡ Collaboration and Teaming Among Early Childhood Professionals and Family Members.

In addition, an annual, statewide Early Intervention Conference is sponsored and supported by several state agencies (e.g., North Carolina Interagency Coordinating Council, Department of Human Resources, and Division of Maternal and Child Health). Collaborative training activities promote and support the sharing of knowledge and competencies among parents and professionals who are involved with young children with developmental delays. In addition, across time, collaborative training fosters the acquisition of common conceptual frameworks for service providers who work with young children with developmental delays. Through collaborative efforts and interagency agreements, personnel working in local agencies and schools are able to access the inservice training needed to maintain high-quality early childhood services.

Several states have also encouraged and developed interagency collaborative agreements on the local levels (Rosenkoetter et al., 1995). Typically, local interagency agreements are less formal than the state agreements and they indicate a willingness of personnel in local agencies to work together in the "best interest" of the children and families that they serve. Often, agreements on the local level facilitate the coordination and provision of services and prevent unnecessary duplication of effort. For example, a child with a visual impairment may also need speech therapy. One local agency may provide services related to the visual impairments and another local agency may provide speech therapy services. Instead of the child going to two different agencies and having two different individualized plans (IEPs), the agency personnel may work collaboratively in developing the child's individualized program and agree to provide any needed related services in an inclusive early childhood program.

Challenges and Benefits of Collaboration

While collaboration is an important goal for service provision in early childhood programs, many challenges are often encountered. When effective collaboration is achieved among parents and professionals, however, services for young children with developmental delays are delivered more effectively.

Challenges of Collaboration

It is advantageous to identify the challenges to collaboration so they can be addressed proactively. Four critical challenges inherent in collaboration are listed and discussed briefly in Table 1.

In order for collaboration to occur, professionals and administrators must be open to working together. Administrators should be supportive of personnel who want to collaborate with other

Four Critical Challenges to Collaboration

1. **Philosophical differences between the various professional disciplines (e.g., physical therapy, early childhood special education, early childhood education, nursing) may make it difficult for collaborating when providing services to young children.** Inherent in philosophical perspectives is each individual's personal values, cultural background, personal experiences, and professional training. For example, physical therapists are typically inculcated with a perspective that is congruent with a traditional medical model for service delivery. Given their perspective, many physical therapists provide services directly to the child and typically focus only of the child's specific motor development needs. Physical therapists who continue to operate within the framework of a tradition medical model will probably not include a child's family in identifying or providing intervention strategies, particularly in home and child care settings. On the other hand, many early childhood special educators are trained to address the needs of the children within the context of the family in home and early childhood settings. Another example of potential philosophical differences might be an early childhood educator who may believe that children learn best through play and exploration and that children do not benefit from teacher-directed learning activities. On the other hand, an early childhood special educator might believe that children with significant developmental delays (e.g., mental retardation, autism) may need (indeed require) a better balance of both child-initiated and teacher-directed activities to promote critical developmental competencies in inclusive preschools (Wolery, Strain, & Bailey, 1992).

2. **The time and training needed for developing team-building skills and relationships, which are essential for effective collaboration, are not typically viewed as priorities and therefore often are not included as part of routine professional development activities.** For example, many professionals working in the field of early childhood special education have a number of children and families to work and plan with and they often find it difficult to schedule time for team building activities (Brown et al., in press). For professionals to collaborate effectively, they need to function well as a team. Moreover effective team functioning is an evolving process that requires professional development activities and time to support collaborative competencies and collaboration (File & Kontos, 1992).

3. **Administrative support for using a collaborative approach in service provision is often lacking.** Administrators may or may not understand the value of the team building process. Therefore, they may not favor the use of financial resources for professional development activities and time resources needed to promote and support professional collaboration (File & Kontos, 1992). For example, an occupational therapist may be hired to provide direct services to young children with fine motor delays. The occupational therapist's role may be restricted to one-to-one direct therapy and may not allow her to meet with and collaborate with other professionals working with children. This service delivery method may well result in a less than optimal program for children and a failure of professionals to collaborate to plan for children with developmental delays.

4. **The provision of services using a collaborative approach becomes difficult because of the diversity of settings and locations of services for young children.** For example, it is a very complex process for professionals from a variety of disciplines to meet regularly and plan children's individualized programs (i.e., IEPs, IFSPs). Indeed, the fact that professionals are often from different disciplines, more than one community agency, and may be geographically distant may inhibit the collaborative processes. Merely, scheduling periodic meetings can become a major challenge to collaborative processes (Brown et al., in press).

Table 1.

professionals providing services to children with developmental delays and supply them with the necessary resources. Similarly, professionals should be willing to commit the time needed to collaborate and be open to different opinions even when they conflict with their own personal beliefs. Making professional changes involves a risk of the unknown, therefore, some professionals may be resistive and unwilling to cooperate beyond their well-defined professional roles (Ryan-Vincek, Tuesday-Heathfred & Lamorey, 1995). Because a commitment to collaborate involves changes in professionals' and administrators' attitudes and behavior, they may not be willing to participate in collaborative processes. Even though there are obstacles to collaboration, this process can be further enhanced when professionals work together to overcome them.

Benefits of Collaboration

While the challenges to collaboration among parents and professionals appear to be significant, the benefits of collaboration can be overwhelmingly positive (e.g., Bailey, 1994; Bruder & Bologna, 1993; Dunst & Paget, 1991; File & Kontos, 1992; Raver, 1991). Children, families and professionals all profit from collaboration.

Benefits for children with developmental delays and their families include better coordinated and integrated services and practical IEP and IFSP goals that are based on transdisciplinary team planning. As a result, these goals can be readily implemented in inclusive preschool programs. A unified philosophy that is developed by a collaborative team ensures professionalism and cohesiveness among professionals who work with children with and without developmental delays (Bruder, 1993). A transdisciplinary approach provides opportunities for professionals and parents to communicate and solve problems. In addition, multiple disciplines focus on children's individual goals and achievement through routine schedule and activities of inclusive preschool programs.

Finally, with adoption of collaborative and transdisciplinary approaches, inservice training will address the needs of team members promote further collaboration and provide coordinated and effective services to children and families (Bruder, 1993). This training would occur across disciplines, thereby, further enhancing the collaborative process. Likewise, a greater understanding of the philosophical differences among professionals would be facilitated.

Agencies may also benefit from collaboration. Many agencies have very limited resources, and by collaborating with professionals in other agencies, a greater array of services can be made available to the families and children (Bruder, 1993). For example, an early childhood special educator may be able to provide assistance to early childhood educators in planning for children who are "at risk" for developmental difficulties (e.g., behavioral problems, language delays) but who have not been identified and are not yet eligible for special education services. In addition, collaboration with professionals in other agencies, particularly in providing coordinated inservice training, might enable administrators to provide richer training opportunities for staff development, thereby enhancing the overall quality of early childhood personnel working in their programs

Strategies for Building Collaborative Partnerships

Collaborative relationships among professionals, agencies, and families are critical for early childhood programs to be effective in serving young children with developmental delays. Partnership is the ultimate goal of collaboration, however, it does not occur without effort. Typically, cooperation (i.e., informal working together) and coordination (i.e., working together on a specific task) precedes collaboration (Foster, 1987). As defined above, collaboration is the commitment to work together for a common goal. Therefore, in early childhood, collaboration occurs when professionals, parents, and agency personnel work together in providing appropriate services that is in the "best interest" of children and their families. A collaborative process emerges when participants have:

➡ common interest in children and their families;

➡ priority for serving children with developmental delays and their families;

➡ genuine trust of other service providers; and

➡ willingness to work together.

Therefore, effective communication and collaborative teamwork are two necessary conditions to promote effective collaboration and partnerships.

Effective Communication

Effective communication is a complex issue. Verbal and nonverbal language, a common knowledge base, cultural awareness, and values may influence communication. Four specific strategies for enhancing communication include:

➡ effective listening skills;

➡ open-ended questions;

➡ nonverbal communication; and

➡ positive perspectives (Rosin, Green, Hecht, Tuchman, & Robbins, 1996).

Effective listening results when we actively attempt to understand the meaning of others' communications. To be an effective listener, one must be attentive and quiet while the other person is talking and wait until they are completely finished before responding. In addition, one needs to understand the feelings the person is trying to communicate with their words. One method to improve listening skills is to partially repeat back what the person said and verify important parts of the message (i.e., active listening). For example, if an early childhood educator and early childhood special educator are developing a child's individual program, it is important that they listen to one another, understand the terminology they are using, ask questions to clarify information or procedures, and respect for others' professional opinions even if they disagree on some aspects of the program. An early childhood educator may explain to an itinerant early childhood special educator that a child with visual impairments is having difficulty adjusting to classroom changes. After listening carefully, the early childhood special educator may rephrase and repeat what the early childhood educator said in an attempt to determine what "difficulties" and what "classroom changes" means for the early childhood educator. Through this process, both professionals are able to clarify information and their thinking and work collaboratively to provide constructive solutions to real or perceived problems.

Thoughtful open-ended questions provide opportunities for individuals to clarify their thoughts and feelings. Often, clarification of individuals' basic assumptions is critical to maintaining effective communication. Open-ended questions are one method to convey to others that you are truly interested in what they have to say. For example, rather than asking, "Does Marissa interact with the other children during center times?" an early childhood special education might say "Tell me about Marissa's interactions with the other children." Furthermore, the use of open-ended questions usually results in more elaborate answers and information than specific questions.

Nonverbal language is important to effective communication. Nonverbal forms of communication that may or may not accompany verbal communication and might include body positioning, facial expressions, eye contact, and attention to the speaker. While one is listening, it is important to maintain a body posture that indicates an interest in what the speaker is saying. For example, if an early childhood educator does not look at the early childhood special educator when they are talking, then the early childhood special educator might assume that the early childhood educator is not interested or not listening. Subtle nonverbal barriers to communication may make collaboration more difficult for adults.

Adopting a positive perspective can promote and enhance interactions among individuals. Even difficult situations can have positive aspects. The perspective one has during a conversation with another person can have a powerful affect on an evolving relationship. For example, if a physical therapist comes into the classroom and simply informs teachers that they have been positioning a child incorrectly, the teachers will probably be less receptive to working with the therapist in the future. Conversely, if the physical therapist approaches teachers with the idea of working together to implement practical procedures to improve a child's classroom participation and then demonstrates appropriate positioning techniques for a child during classroom activities, teachers may be more willing to implement appropriate positioning when the therapist is not present in their classroom. Furthermore, teachers will be more likely to communicate and collaborate with the physical therapist in the future. In another example, if teachers, regardless of their intention, make negative comments to parents about their children, they may inhibit future parent-teacher communication. Specifically, their negative communications may cause parents to become defensive, or feel the teacher does not like their children, or become hostile with teachers. On the other hand, if teachers frequently discuss the positive characteristics and traits of children with the parents, across time a good parent-teacher relationship will evolve. After the relationship has emerged, teachers will be in a better position to talk candidly with parents about potential problems and potential solutions to those problems. In addition, teachers should solicit parental perspectives on the nature of the problem and possible solutions. With this thoughtful approach and a positive perspective, parents will be less likely to be reactive and negative with teachers and more willing to communicate openly with children's service providers.

Collaborative Teamwork

The concept of a transdisciplinary team implies that members are working together to solve common problems and make decisions (Rosin et al., 1996). Teamwork is an intricate process that involves an understanding of group processes and personal commitments of time and energy. Successful teamwork includes:

- a clear purpose and shared vision for team members;
- mutual trust and respect for others;
- open and honest communication among team members;
- a recognition of others' different opinions; and
- a willingness to understand others' perspectives (Jesien, 1996; Quick, 1992).

Teamwork can be both challenging and rewarding. The ultimate strength of teaming is the involvement of team members in the decision process and the shared acceptance of the group decisions.

An effective team evolves over time. Initially, team members get to know one another and begin to understand their different perspectives. As a team develops, common goals and informal guidelines for working together are established as well as the roles and responsibilities of each team members are defined. Because team building is a growth process that emerges across time, team membership should be as stable as possible. When membership changes, team dynamics are usually different, and the process of team building and functioning must begin again. When team membership is relatively consistent, however, orientation of new members will be easier and team functioning will be compatible.

While team members work together for common goals, the major activity they engage in is problem-solving. Although teams take different approaches to problem-solving, techniques for effective problem-solving have similar components. One technique, the BRIDGE model (Prentice & Spencer, 1986) includes five steps:

- identifying the problem and collecting relevant information;
- "brainstorming" to identify possible solutions;
- reviewing the merits of possible solutions;
- implementing an agreed upon solution; and
- evaluating the success of the agreed upon solution. A structured team process promotes team members' careful examination of problems and solutions and may enable members to be more effective participants in the problem-solving process.

An example of the BRIDGE model for problem solving is illustrated next. Karley, a three-year-old with a visual impairment is not making progress on her IEP goals. Step one of the BRIDGE model would include identification of the problem and fact finding. For example, team members might:

- discuss Karley's lack of progress in accomplishing her IEP objectives;
- review recent assessment information as well as the current teaching strategies implemented;
- discuss with the parents any changes at home that might affect her progress; and

➡solicit relevant information from professionals working directly with Karley. Step two would be to "brainstorm" solutions to the problem (i.e., lack of progress on IEP goals) with team members.

For example, team members might suggest:
- using different teaching strategies
- providing individualized and specialized attention for some activities
- using different activities to facilitate IEP goals.

Step three would be discussing the feasibility of each possible solution. The first solution might be relatively easy to implement in her classroom but Karley may not respond positively to changes. Another solution might be to provide an additional teaching assistant for some of the classroom activities or to have a vision consultant show teachers how to better adapt materials and activities for Karley. This solution, however, may be expensive and the new assistant may require additional training and support to work with a child who has a visual impairment. The third solution might provide for implementation of high-interest activities to motivate Karley to work on her IEP goals without incurring additional expenses. However, more creative planning would be required by service providers to implement this solution. Step four of the BRIDGE process includes implementing the agreed upon solution. In this case, teachers would implement Karley's IEP goals within the context of activities that are motivating for her. Step five, monitoring the solution might require teachers to collect more frequent assessment information on Karley's progress during the motivating activities. The purpose of the additional assessment information will be for the team members to monitor progress on her IEP goals. If she continues to have problems while participating in classroom activities and is not making progress toward her IEP objectives, the team will need to reactivate the problem-solving process and perhaps revisit some of the more costly solutions to resolving the problem.

In summary, clear and open communication and cooperative teamwork are effective strategies for enhancing the collaborative process in programs serving young children with and without developmental delays. These strategies need to be thoughtfully planned for and practiced in order for team members to become effective in the collaborative team development process. In addition, they should be encouraged and facilitated by administrators and professional peers.

Conclusion

Young children with developmental delays are served by a number of disciplines in different agencies in a variety of settings. For services to be provided in a coherent and consistent manner, they must be coordinated. Family members may assume a service coordination role, and early childhood special educators or other early childhood professionals often provide critical aspects of and support for service coordination. Professionals and parents should be wise consumers of the services and resources needed to enhance and support children with developmental delays and their families. Because of the involvement of multiple individuals, collaboration and team approaches to planning and implementing services for young children with developmental delays is the most effective method of service coordination. For children in inclusive preschool programs, early childhood educators should become proactive team members along with other service providers needed to provide high-quality early childhood services. When collaboration and service coordination among professionals, families, and agencies transpires, the overall quality of early childhood services improves, and the overall quality of the lives of our young children and their families is enhanced.

References

Bailey, D. M. (1994). Working with families of children with special needs. In M. Wolery & J. S. Wilbers (Eds.), *Including children with special needs in early childhood programs* (pp. 23-44). Washington, DC: National Association for the Education of Young Children.

Bailey, D. B., Simeonsson, R. J., Yoder, D. E., & Huntington, G. S. (1990). Preparing professionals to serve infants and toddlers with handicaps and their families: An integrative analysis across eight disciplines. *Exceptional Children, 57*, 26-35.

Bloch, J. S., & Seitz, M. (1989). Parents as assessors of children: A collaborative approach to helping. *Social Work in Education*, 226-244.

Brown, W. H., Horn, E. M., Heiser, J. G., & Odom, S. L. (in press). Project BLEND: An inclusive model of early intervention services. *Journal of Early Intervention*.

Bruder, M. B. (1993). The provision of early intervention and early childhood special education within community early childhood programs: Characteristics of effective service delivery. *Topics in Early Childhood Special Education, 13*(1), 19-37.

Bruder, M. B., & Bologna, T. (1993). Collaboration and service coordination for effective early intervention. In W. B. Brown, S. K. Thurman, & L. F. Pearl (Eds.), *Family-centered early intervention with infants and toddlers: Innovative cross-disciplinary approaches* (pp. 103-127). Baltimore: Paul H. Brookes.

DEC Task Force on Recommended Practices. (1993). *DEC recommended practices: Indicators of quality in programs for infants and young children with special needs and their families*. Reston, VA: The Council for Exceptional Children.

Dunst, C. J., & Paget, K. D. (1991). Parent-professional partnerships and family empowerment. In M. J. Fine (Ed.), *Collaboration with parents of exceptional children* (pp. 25-44). Brandon, VT: Clinical Psychology Publishing.

Dunst, C. J., & Trivette, C. M. (1989). An enablement and empowerment perspective of case management. *Topics in Early Childhood Special Education, 8*(4), 87-102.

Dunst, C. J., Trivette, C. M., & Deal, A. G. (1994). Enabling and empowering families. In C. J. Dunst, C. M. Trivette, & A. G. Deal (Eds.), *Supporting & strengthening families: Methods, strategies and practice* (pp. 2-11). Cambridge, MA: Brookline Books.

Eagen, C., Petisi, M., & Tools, A. (1980). *The transdisciplinary training, assessment, and consultation model preschool program: A regional demonstration program for preschool handicapped children*. Yorktown Heights, NY: Putnam and Northern Westchester Counties Board of Cooperative Educational Services.

File, N., & Kontos, S. (1992). Indirect service delivery through consultation: Review and implications for early intervention. *Journal of Early Intervention, 16*(3), 221-233.

Foster, G. W. (1987). Abstracts of presented papers and the proceedings of the Association of Teachers in Science. *North Central Region and Society for College Science Teachers Conference*, (1986, October 29-30).

Jesien, G. S. (1996). Interagency collaboration: What, why, and with whom. In P. Rosin, A. D. Whitehead, L. I. Tuchman, G. S. Jesien, A. L. Begun, & L. Irwin (Eds.), *Partnerships in family-centered care: A guide to collaborative early intervention*. Baltimore: Paul H. Brookes.

Leviton, A., Mueller, M., & Kauffman, C. (1992). The family-centered consultation model: Practical application for professionals. *Infants and Children, 4*(3), 1-8.

Linder, T. (1993). *Transdisciplinary play-based assessment: A functional approach to working with young children*. Baltimore: Paul H. Brookes.

McGonigel, M. J., & Garland, C. W. (1988). The Individualized Family Service Plan and the early intervention team: Team and family issues and recommended practices. *Infants and Young Children, 1*(1), 10-21.

North Carolina Interagency Coordinating

Council (1994, February). *Annual Report to the Honorable Governor James B. Hunt Regarding Services For Children With Or At Risk For Disabilities Ages Birth To Five And Their Families In The State Of North Carolina*. Raleigh, North Carolina. Author.

Odom, S. L., & McLean, M. E. (Eds.). (1996). *Early intervention/early childhood special education: Recommended practices*. Austin, TX: PRO-ED.

Orelove, F .P., & Sobsey, D. (1987). *Educating children with multiple disabilities: A transdisciplinary approach*. Baltimore: Paul H. Brooks.

Prentice, R. R., & Spencer, P. E. (1986). *Project Bridge; decision-making for early services: A team approach*. Chicago, IL: American Academy of Pediatrics.

Public Law 94-142. (1975). *Education for All Handicapped Children's Act*. Washington, DC.

Public Law 99-457. (1986). *Amendments to Education for All Handicapped Children's Act*. Washington, DC.

Public Law 101-576. (1990). *Individuals With Disabilities Education Act*. Washington, DC.

Public Law 102-119. (1991). *Amendments to the Individuals With Disabilities Education Act*. Washington, DC.

Public Law 105-17. (1997). *Individuals With Disabilities Education Act Amendments of 1997*. Washington, DC.

Quick, T. (1992). *Successful team building*. New York: AMACOM, a division of American Management Association.

Rainforth, B., York, J., & MacDonald, C. (1992). *Collaborative teams for students with severe disabilities: Integrating therapy and educational services*. Baltimore: Paul H. Brookes.

Raver, S. A. (1991). *Strategies for teaching at-risk and handicapped infants and toddlers: A transdisciplinary approach*. New York: Merrill.

Rosenkoetter, S. E., Shotts, C. K., Streufert, C. A., Rosenkoetter, L. I., Campbell, M., & Torrez, J. (1995). Local Interagency Coordination Councils as infrastructure for early intervention: One state's implementation. *Topics in Early Childhood Special Education, 15*(3), 264-280.

Rosin, P., Green, M., Hecht, L., Tuchman, L., & Robins, S. (1996). *Pathways: A training and resource guide for enhancing skills in early intervention service coordination*. Madison, WI: Waisman Center at the University of Wisconsin-Madison.

Ryan-Vincek, S., Tuesday-Heathfield, L., & Lamorey, S. (1995). From theory to practice: A pilot study of team members' perspectives on transdisciplinary service delivery. *Infant-Toddler Intervention, 5*(2), 153-176.

Shelton, T., & Stepanek, J. (1994). *Family-centered care for children needing specialized health and developmental services*. Bethesda, MD: Association for the Care of Children's Health.

Swick, K. J. (1993). *Empowering at-risk families during the early childhood years*. Washington, DC: National Education Association of the United States.

Turnbull, A. P., & Turnbull, H. R., III. (1990). *Families, professionals, and exceptionality: A special partnership* (Second Ed.). New York: Macmillan.

Wesley, P. W. (1994). Innovative practices: Providing on-site consultation to promote quality in integrated child care programs. *Journal of Early Intervention, 18*(4) 391-402.

Weil, M., & Karls, J. M. (1989). *Case management in human service practice*. San Francisco: Jossey-Bass Publishers.

Winton, P. J. (1986). The developmentally delayed child within the family context. In B. Keogh (Ed.), *Advances in special education* (Vol. 5, pp. 219-256).

Wolery, M., Strain, P. S., & Bailey, D. B. (1992). Reaching potentials of children with special needs. In S. Bredekamp & T. Rosegrant (Eds.) *Reaching potentials: Appropriate curriculum and assessment for young children* (pp. 92-111). Washington, DC: National Association for the Education of Young Children.

CHAPTER 3

Activity-based Intervention Strategies for Serving Young Children with Developmental Delays in Early Childhood Programs

Juliann Woods Cripe
and
Julia M. Lee
Valdosta State University
Department of Special Education and Communication Disorders
Valdosta, GA

"A physically responsive environment will encourage exploratory independence and success." (Leister, 1996, p. 25)

It is hot outside! The three- and four-year-olds do not really notice the heat and are enthusiastically playing on the playground. The playground is always a favorite for children at the child care center because of the activity choices available. The swings are popular. The movement of the swing makes a little bit of air move. The slides, the sand and water tables, and the trucks are also favorites.

Mary Catherine and her friend, Heather, choose the swings. They are enjoying the air they feel. It makes their long hair blow across their faces. While Mary Catherine is swinging high, Heather is next to her singing, "I have a friend and her name is Mary Catherine ..." Mary Catherine looks at Heather and smiles widely.

The children are back in the classroom in small groups, getting ready for center time. Photographs of the centers are available for use during the planning phase. Ms. Stephanie asks Mary Catherine, "Which centers do you want to visit?" Mary Catherine looks at the photograph choices and reaches toward the picture of blocks and the art center. Her choices made, she watches as her friends make their decisions.

At the art center, Christie asks Mary Catherine to join her in painting a picture together. Each selects a paint color and begins. Christie takes Mary Catherine's right arm and helps her reach and grasp her paint sponge which is placed on her left side. Christie and Mary Catherine giggle together as they paint. Each takes several turns reaching and dipping the sponge into the paint and back to the paper. They use many different colors.

It's been a busy morning, and now it's lunchtime! The children get ready to go to the dining room. Ms. Stephanie helps Mary Catherine get her toy shopping cart to walk with the other children. "Goodness, what hungry children!" comments Ms. Stephanie, "everyone is ready to go to lunch."

During lunch, Mary Catherine chooses water to drink (she really doesn't like the apple juice that is offered). Ms. Stephanie places her drink to Mary Catherine's left. Her cup has handles, and Heather helps her reach and grasp the cup the way Ms. Stephanie showed her to do. Heather and Mary Catherine giggle when Heather lifts her cup to touch Mary Catherine's cup in a toast. Heather tells Mary Catherine that she has seen her Grandpa do that with his glass.

This scenario is very typical for young children because children having fun while learning through play, active exploration, social interaction, organized group activities, and daily routines is the foundation of early childhood education. Mary Catherine, Heather, and Christie enjoy playing with each other and their other friends at the child care center, while learning new skills. Ms. Stephanie, the teacher, and her assistant arrange the classroom and playground to create many opportunities for the children to develop new skills and practice previously learned ones. The adults at the center participate in the activities to support the process of learning from and playing with friends.

Friends are important to Mary Catherine. She looks forward to seeing her friends and participating in the activities at the center. Indeed, one of her favorite activities is smiling and interacting with others. Mary Catherine, age 4, has been diagnosed with cerebral palsy. She moves about by crawling and is learning to walk behind a small shopping cart. She communicates through facial expressions, vocalizations, and by making choices with her eye gaze. Mary Catherine works on skills she needs to learn throughout the day while playing with her friends, participating in the same types of activities and following the schedule of daily routines.

Look back at the scenario now and see how Mary Catherine was actually "working" on the skills identified on her Individualized Education Plan (IEP), the program of services developed by her education team. She used her eye gaze and reach to communicate her choices to swing, to go to the art center, and to drink water. She practiced walking with the shopping cart on the way to the playground and back, and to and from the lunch room. By placing objects to Mary's side, she was able to practice reaching across midline and grasping objects during art and at lunch. She used "tools" when she painted pictures at the art center with sponges and when she used her shopping cart. And finally, she worked on cup drinking without hyperextending her head at lunch.

Activity-based Intervention

The approach used to support Mary Catherine's learning is known as activity-based intervention (Bricker & Cripe, 1992). Activity-based intervention (ABI) has been defined as a child-directed, transactional approach that embeds intervention on children's individual goals and objectives in routine, planned, or child-initiated activities. In addition, teachers and care givers who employ ABI use logically occurring antecedents and consequences to develop functional and generalizable skills (Bricker & Cripe, 1992). What this really means is that for young children with identified disabilities, like Mary Catherine, ABI provides a framework for developing and implementing individualized intervention within developmentally appropriate preschool and child care programs.

ABI is not a curriculum kit or set of specific instructional strategies. Rather, it is an approach based on principles that allows flexibility in accommodating a variety of needs for individual children. For example, the plan developed for Mary Catherine is different from one that would be developed for a child with specific communication delays such as difficult to understand speech or immature language. It is also different from a plan that would be developed for a younger or older child, a child with different interests, or for a child whose family had different priorities. Because ABI is a flexible framework and not a specific content or set of instructional sequences, it fosters individualization based on children's identified developmental needs, families' values and goals, and children's interest in people, materials, and activities. Moreover, the flexibility of ABI allows for individualization needed within routines and schedules within preschool and child care programs as well as any specific accommodations necessary for children with developmental delays.

ABI provides the organization necessary to support children with developmental delays within a variety of preschool and child care programs. The principles necessary for successful implementation of ABI are common to high-quality early childhood programs including child-directed learning, responsive adult interactions, environments and materials that foster active engagement and exploration, and a comprehensive curriculum guided by a developmental model (Bredekamp, 1987; Bruder, 1996). In addition, ABI assures that children with developmental delays have the support necessary to achieve skills within early childhood programs by planning specific goals and objectives and monitoring progress in learning through on-going observation and assessment. Individualized strategies are identified for practicing the skills embedded throughout the children's schedules within the existing early childhood curriculum.

Instructional planning by a team of family members, care providers, teachers, and therapists occurs to ensure sufficient teaching and learning opportunities are provided. ABI shares many theoretical and philosophical tenets with early childhood education, but it also encompasses the recommended practices of early childhood special education making it an effective and efficient approach to use with young children with developmental delays in preschool and child care programs (Wolery & Sainato, 1996). It combines a behavior analytic approach known for its effectiveness in teaching individuals with disabilities with effective early childhood principles (Bailey, 1996).

ABI is designed to take advantage of children's natural environments. It is an approach that disperses training of specific skills throughout the day as opportunities arise within authentic activities rather than in an intense, structured training setting. Almost any activity that occurs within early childhood settings can be an opportunity for learning to occur (Kostelnik, Colker, & Dodge, 1993). Within an ABI approach, "activity" refers to a sequence of events that has an identifiable beginning and a logical outcome. Within an activity, opportunities exist for the children to initiate and practice a variety of skills or behaviors. To encourage a systematic analysis of potential learning opportunities, activities within children's routine day are divided into child-initiated, routine or planned activities (Bricker & Cripe, 1992). Child-initiated activities are defined as those in which children identify materials or activities such as playing in the household center or building with blocks. Routines are the common predictable events in children's lives such as meals, clean up, dressing and undressing. Activities planned for the purpose of intervention (planned ABI activities) would not necessarily occur without adult involvement and organization. For example, with adult assistance and support, art projects, games, planting seeds, or acting out a story can be organized to provide teaching and learning opportunities for promoting important developmental skills. The following example of Kathryn illustrates how intervention can be embedded throughout the day within child-initiated play, typical daily routines, and within planned activities.

It's center time at Head Start. Kathryn and Shaniqua are at the housekeeping area. Shaniqua says to Kathryn, "Please give me the apron." Kathryn looks confused. Shaniqua points to the apron, and Kathryn hands it to her. "Thanks, Kathryn," Shaniqua says, "What do you want?" Kathryn looks at the frying pan and verbalizes. "Here," says Shaniqua.

Everyone washes up after play time to get ready for lunch. Kathryn carefully adjusts the water and begins to wash her hands. Ms. Pat laughs with Kathryn about the soap bubbles while she says "pop" and "bubbles." Ms. Pat tells her to make mittens on her hands with the soap so she is sure to get all the dirt off. Kathryn turns to Dionté and shows him "my mittens." Dionté responds by joining Kathryn to make "more mittens."

It's story time. The children are in a circle on the floor so that each can see the book. Ms. Pat has chosen a book today that is about a bear family, including mama bear, papa bear and baby bear going on a picnic. Kathryn is sitting across from Ms. Pat so that she can see the book clearly and watch Ms. Pat's mouth as she pronounces the words. There are many opportunities in the story for Kathryn to hear p, b, and m sounds, the sounds she is working on with her speech clinician. Ms. Pat repeats the answers Kathryn gives providing another opportunity for Kathryn to hear the correct pronunciation and to clarify her response for the children who might not have understood her.

The definitions of child-initiated, routine and planned activities are not mutually exclusive, nor are they intended to be. In essence, an underlying objective of every activity should be to provide children with the opportunities to initiate actions so the adults can follow their interests and motivation. Thus children's active engagement with materials and others will provide many teaching and learning opportunities. In the hand washing sequence, Ms. Pat was prepared to embed opportunities for Kathryn to hear and say the words bubbles, pop, and mittens. When Kathryn initiated the interaction with Dionté to show her mittens, additional opportunities for practice were generated within the routine.

These examples of child-initiated, routine and planned activities share several important features. First and foremost, they are authentic, meaningful activities that make sense to children and are likely to occur frequently throughout the day in many situations. Dramatic play, story time, and self-care routines are standard activities in homes and early childhood centers, and those activities are of interest to many children. Second, activities that are interesting or that involve interesting materials reduce or eliminate the need for artificial rewards or praise. Children engage in these activities because they want to or because it is an means to an end (e.g., washing hands after outdoor play is required before beginning to play in the centers) not because they receive artificial rewards. High-interest activities support child engagement by reducing the need for adult involvement in the activities. Children continue practicing skills not because adults tell them to, but because they are enjoying it. Third, high-interest activities usually occur in natural contexts with family and friends, and those social contexts encourage social interaction. Developing and supporting skills in typical situations and with children and adults in those common settings should result in efficient and effective learning (Wolery & Sainato, 1996). By using common and frequently occurring activities, repetition, a fourth key feature, provides many additional opportunities for practice and learning. Repetition is an essential feature for young children's effective learning. Finally, child-directed, routine, and planned activities are dynamic and flexible. These activities can be varied according to children's specific needs and developmental level, and they can be made more challenging and difficult as children's developmental repertoires becomes more elaborate and sophisticated. The following sections provide further information on the utility of child-initiated, routine and planned activities for implementation of ABI for children with developmental delays in early childhood programs.

Child-Initiated Activities and Play

Play is a central organizing framework for early cognitive, social, and language development (Piaget, 1962; Vygotsky, 1962) that stimulates and supports development in all of the learning domains (Smilansky & Shefatya, 1990; Fewell & Vadasy, 1983; Garvey, 1977; Vygotsky, 1967). During play, children are likely to initiate activities that can actually serve as a context for intervention. When intervention is embedded into play using preferred materials, children will maintain interest, practice skills without the need for adult reinforcement, and will use the skills in a meaningful context (Kostelnik, Soderman, & Whiren, 1993). Because children have different play interests and styles, team members must get to know children individually as an initial step for planning intervention (Martin, 1994). Some children meet each play opportunity with enthusiasm, while others are thoughtful and methodical, enjoying the taste, touch, and look of each material. Child-initiated play is a valuable learning activity for young children, and should be an integral part of each child's day (Kostelnik et al., 1993). Play provides enjoyment for both children and their care providers, opportunities to explore objects and construct experiences within the environment, opportunities to interact and negotiate with peers, and it facilitates acquisition of important skills and competencies across developmental domains (Koralek et al., 1993).

Play is also a very effective intervention strategy. For example, Kathryn loves to play. No one ever has to ask her to go play! She comes in the door of the classroom each morning, drops her things in her cubby and is off to play with her friends. She especially enjoys dramatic play and dressing up. Her friends may not always understand what she is saying but they interact with her by using the objects from the dramatic play center and her actions to predict or interpret her meaning. Dramatic play facilitates social interaction and communication with her age mates. Kathryn has multiple opportunities to communicate with and to receive feedback from her friends. She hears the words spoken and is motivated to be an effective communicator in order to continue playing with peers. Low structure activities, such as most play activities, provide more communicative exchanges between young children than structured activities like circle or story time (Wolery, 1994). In Kathryn's case, play activities made an excellent context to implement her intervention plan.

Play may require adaptations for some children with developmental delays (Wolery & Wilbers, 1994). Mary Catherine's physical disabilities do not preclude her play, but do necessitate environmental arrangements. She is most comfortable in a swing with a sturdy back and sides that supports her in an upright position and allows her to maintain face-to-face contact with her friends. Because her movements are slow and lack precise control, she needs soft hand-sized blocks in the block corner that are easy for her grasp and a container with a large opening to place them in for storage initially. As her motor control improves, she will be able to handle different textures, sizes and shapes and place them in containers with a controlled release. Mary Catherine also uses switches for battery operated toys and has a special keyboard for the computer. In the classroom, some spaces need to be open so Mary Catherine can dance to the music while in her wheelchair. She walks with her shopping cart to the grocery store where she selects her groceries and puts them in the cart. Play is the special work of young children because it gives them the opportunity for success (Rogers & Sawyers, 1988). Supporting young children with special needs to play requires that the adults arrange the environment and the materials to assure that success occurs (Cook, Tessier, & Klein, 1996).

Daily Routines

Daily routines provide additional opportunities for the development of children's skills and for practicing emerging skills. By definition, routines occur both regularly and frequently, and as such they provide young children and their care providers with a variety of opportunities to engage in specifically planned skills or activities. These routines may include eating, washing hands, quiet play and naptime, potty time, getting ready for going home, or any other formally defined or informally identified activity sequences. Because teachers and care givers organize routines within their programs and those common activities already exist in early childhood programs, the use of daily routines as contexts for children's interventions may be the easiest for early childhood personnel to implement initially. Using existing routines does not require additional staff members or materials, nor does it interfere with the ongoing responsibilities (Wolery, 1994).

Routines provide opportunities for children's teachers and care givers to participate in intervention. As team members work together with families to deliver services in a variety of settings, it is essential that the importance of the daily routines in the lives of children and their families is given proper consideration. Obviously, daily routines will differ dramatically from child to child, from family to family, from one setting to another, and, perhaps, from one week to the next. Planning interventions within routines at early childhood programs that cannot be continued within homes or that conflict with families' values is not good practice because it can confuse children and inhibit learning and may reduce trust and collaboration between families and teachers. For example, if Kathryn's Grandmother, her primary care provider, did not believe it was appropriate to play in the sink while washing her hands, then asking her to pop bubbles and make soap mittens to provide opportunities for Kathryn to practice her "p," "b," and "m" sounds would not be good practice.

To integrate intervention into existing routines, it is necessary to identify specific routines that exist, and their frequency. Most settings, including home or preschool environments, have a relatively regular schedule of activities. The sequence of activities and the precision of the schedule will vary greatly depending upon the care provider's philosophy and the staff ratio. One of the first steps is to identify the activities that occur within a typical day. This is usually a fairly straightforward procedure and can be accomplished by teachers or care providers listing the events in which children participate in the order in which they occur.

A commonly used strategy to facilitate planning is to then take this schedule of activities and use it in the development of an intervention schedule or matrix (Bricker & Cripe, 1992; Noonan & McCormick, 1993). The left hand column of the matrix identifies the activities, their location and approximate times for the activity. Across the top of the matrix, the specific child targets are listed in columns. Within the cells of the matrix, the team identifies which skills will be addressed in each activity. Sometimes it is helpful within the matrix cell to identify specific strategies or materials to be used, the proposed number of opportunities planned, or the person responsible for working with and monitoring children. If opportunities are not planned to practice a specific skill within an activity, then that cell of the matrix is left empty (Wolery, 1994).

The development of a schedule matrix provides a visual reminder of the objectives to be addressed, as well as when and where they will be addressed throughout children's day. It can also serve as a valuable form of communication between the team members, family members, teachers, care providers, speech language therapists, physical or occupational therapists who work with children. The schedule matrix can assist in planning as well as in documentation of the number and types of opportunities planned. It can be helpful for both care providers at home and in group settings. It is especially useful when multiple care givers and team members at different settings are involved in children's programs. The team can see at a glance when an objective is not being addressed frequently enough or when additional or different routines or activities need to be developed to support progress and generalization.

Early childhood special educators can use the schedule matrix to support inclusion because it shows how the schedule already developed at the child care or preschool is used to embed intervention. Developing a schedule matrix with child care providers or teachers helps to reassure them that interventions for children with developmental delays will not add significantly more work, but rather use activities that are already occurring. Team members from different disciplines can use the schedule matrix as a starting point for integrating therapies such as speech and language and physical therapy. They can each identify preferred times and activities for embedding specific skills throughout the day and decide how multiple objectives across developmental domains can be incorporated into the same routine or activity.

Embedding intervention into the routines requires identifying opportunities for practice of skills during each routine. As an example, consider Katrina, age three, who is working on following one-step directions and using a refined grasp. During her busy morning in the center, she has many opportunities to help Ms. Mattie to pick up the blocks, to feed herself Cheerios, apple chunks and raisins at breakfast, to get her diaper and wipes for changing, and to dance to songs during circle time. While Ms. Mattie is setting up the art materials for some other children, Katrina is busy playing with her friend, Matt, sorting toys from the buckets. Katrina and Matt work at taking all the cars and trucks out of the buckets. The size and shape of the vehicles vary and require Katrina and Matt to use different grasping strategies to successfully empty the containers. Ms. Mattie joins them and provides directions on putting the cars and trucks away again so everyone can go outside. On the playground, Katrina joins a "Simon Says" game led by Ms. Mattie, and then swings for a while. Next she goes to the sand box and picks up little rocks and puts them in a pail. Later, she takes them indoors and puts them in a clear plastic container full of her "rock collection" from the playground.

Throughout the course of the morning, Katrina has had more than 50 opportunities to practice her grasp and 15 different opportunities to follow one-step directions. Moreover, one-step directions are important because many of those requests are directly related to participating in her preschool activities. How did all this practice occur when Ms. Mattie was so busy with all the children and not just Katrina?

First, the team had observed Katrina and knew that she preferred to play with the blocks and other hand-sized objects she could stack and sort, push and pile around her. She enjoyed playing in the sand on the playground and finding the rocks which she would carefully pick up and examine. Ms. Mattie reported that Katrina liked to eat her cereal dry and drink her milk separately, and that she tended to finger feed more than using her spoon. Ms. Mattie shared that her favorite group times included circle games, records with actions, and reading short stories. By examining the typical schedule, Katrina's preferred activities and Ms. Mattie's group times, opportunities for Katrina were easily identified. Adding some additional appropriate finger foods to her meals, a few more toys to the containers, and initiating a rock collection provided many additional opportunities for practicing grasping objects. Ms. Mattie was able to give Katrina simple directions to follow during self-care activities without decreasing her time with other children. By identifying teaching and learning opportunities during circle games and music, Ms. Mattie was able to ensure Katrina had turns offered to her and that she participated appropriately.

When teaching and learning opportunities are to be embedded into naturally occurring events, they must be provided in ways that are non-disruptive to established routines yet frequent enough to assure learning will occur. Activities and routines can be modified in several ways to facilitate the embedding of different learning objectives (Wolery, 1994, Bricker & Cripe, 1992). Materials can often be introduced within routines, and those routines will increase opportunities for practice. For example, raisins and apple chunks were added to Katrina's breakfast foods to give her more opportunities to practice using a refined grasp. Books, songs, and fingerplays can be selected to emphasize different language or articulation skills, motor skills, and social interactions. Novel materials, such as the addition of cowboy hats and boots to the dress up corner, bread and cheese slices cut out in shapes or holiday patterns using cookie cutters, or multicolored floating fish in the water table, may promote increased interest and participation.

There are also many strategies that may be used in routines to facilitate children's initiations and engagement with materials and others within early childhood settings. Specific strategies include the placement of materials just out of children's reach, giving smaller portions of desired materials, or "forgetting" to provide the necessary materials. These "sabotage" strategies can be used within routines to increase the opportunities children have to practice their planned learning objectives. For example, placing Katrina's rock collection on a shelf where she can see it will provide an opportunity for her to request the jar for her new additions when she comes in from recess. Giving Mary Catherine small amounts of water or only tiny pushes on the swing will result in her vocal requests for more water or additional pushes on the swing. When applied skillfully, these strategies will offer additional teaching and learning opportunities without detracting from regular activities, disrupting children's initiations, or interfering with the logical sequence and predictability of classroom routines.

Planned Activities

Planned activities are those activities that would probably not occur without adult initiation (Bricker & Cripe, 1992). For young children, planned activities typically involve art or drama projects, cooking, sand and water science activities, or dress up role play. Planned activities may include obstacle courses and hiking trails, shopping for groceries, fishing and camping trips, playdoh, and building cars and roads with boxes and blocks (Bredekamp, 1987; Koralek, et al., 1993). Water table (or sink) activities will include pouring and squeezing, measuring, and mixing. While an integral component of the general curriculum for all children, planned activities also should focus on the children's specific learning objectives for maximum developmental progress to occur.

When planning activities, it is critical to focus on children's learning objectives and not to become too detailed or specific with the activity. For example, making pudding provides many opportunities for turn taking, following directions, measuring and pouring, as well as many communicative and social interactions. The high-interest activity is completed quickly, the results are good to eat, and it can be repeated often. On the other hand, making a three-layer applecake, while a novel experience for most children, is quite complicated and takes significantly longer than instant pudding! The process is much more important than the product. Intricately planned activities or those that require following specific instructions often require extensive adult direction that prohibits following the children's lead. Planned activities for young children will necessitate flexibility and are frequently subject to immediate changes in order to follow children's leads. For example, Kathryn and her friends were busy in the household center fixing lunch for their babies. Ms. Pat planned to model the names of the foods she had placed in the kitchen that morning (potatoes, pop, meat, macaroni, bacon, and buns) to provide opportunities for Kathryn to hear her sounds. Just as the food was being served, three classmates "drove" up in the car they had built from a cardboard box. Kathryn and her friends joined the children in the car for a ride. Following Kathryn's interests, Ms. Pat joined the children as they drove over to the TV corner where Johnny suggested they all go to the movies. Ms. Pat offered pretend popcorn, pop, and a choice of a Bugs Bunny or Mickey Mouse movie. By following Kathryn, Ms. Pat encouraged her interactions with her classmates, who were Kathryn's preferred communication partners. Ms. Pat was able to provide the same number of opportunities as she had planned, just different ones within ongoing classroom activities. She avoided Kathryn's disappointment or feelings of being different by joining the group instead of requiring Kathryn to complete the activity that had been planned. Both routines and planned activities need to be flexible and responsive to unexpected changes that result from child initiations or peer interactions in early childhood settings. Children know their interests best and will indicate their preferences with their behavior. Moreover, they will be highly motivated and more likely to learn during activities they enjoy.

Children with developmental delays may not be able to participate independently in some typical preschool activities, but that doesn't mean that they can not participate at all! An instructional approach known as "partial participation" can be very valuable for children like Mary Catherine with more significant developmental delays. In this approach, the task, such as drinking from a cup, is broken down into a series of smaller steps or subskills. The number of subskills and their complexity is generally dependent upon children's physical and cognitive abilities. In cup drinking, Mary Catherine first opened her mouth as the cup was brought to her lips by her care provider. She held the cup using both hands with the care provider's assistance. With the care provider's physical assistance she returned the cup to the table. Although she can not eat snack independently, using partial participation procedures, she joins her peers at snack in a meaningful way while developing the skills necessary to increase participation and independence.

In a painting with sponges planned activity, Christie helped Mary Catherine participate by gently holding her arm to stabilize and provide the motor control necessary for painting a picture. All activities afford some level of participation by children with developmental delays. Rather than assuming the activity is "too difficult," team members should identify the aspects of activities in which children can participate, thus enhancing not only the children's physical inclusion, but their social and instructional inclusion in early childhood settings (Odom & McEvoy, 1988).

During planned activities, teaching and learning opportunities can often be increased by team analyses of activity sequences. Many hidden opportunities can be found during the set-up and clean-up of the area or activity. Adults can involve children in the gathering and organizing of the materials for snack, the choosing of clothing to put on or the pick up of the toys after play. Care givers must be careful to not preempt opportunities for children to practice skills in routine activities. Adult preempting can easily occur because of the desire to be helpful to children, to be efficient and move on to another task rapidly, or because setting up and cleaning up are traditionally teacher duties. Unfortunetly, preempting may inhibit children's development of independence and their attempts to practice and elaborate many emerging skills.

Whereas early education team members should strive to plan for a balance between play, routines, and planned activi-

Resources for Implementing Activity-based Intervention

Books

Bredekamp, S., & Rosegrant, T. (Eds.). (1992). Reaching potentials: Appropriate curriculum and assessment for young children (Vol.1). Washington: National Association for the Education of Young Children.
> Appropriate assessment and transformational curriculum that enables children to connect learning experiences to conceptual development discussed with examples. Efficacy of developmental/learning continuum for maximum potential explained, including children with special needs, multiculural and linguistically diverse children.

Bricker, D., & Cripe, J. (1992). An activity-based approach to early intervention. Baltimore: Paul H. Brookes.
> Conceptual foundation for activity-based intervention explained. How to embed training in routine, planned, or child-initiated activities and monitor child progress described with examples.

Coling, M. C., & Garrett, J. N. (1995). Activity-based intervention guide. Tucson: The Psychological Corporation.
> Brief introduction to activity-based intervention with hundreds of ideas for activities. Includes suggestions for adapting to special needs children, along with methods for monitoring.

Dolinar, K., Boser, C., & Holm, E. (1994). Learning through play: Curriculum and activities for the inclusive classroom. Albany, NY: Delmar Publishers Inc.
> Brief description of various disabilities and delays with guides for appropriate curriculum. Theme based activities with adaption suggestions for special needs includes resources and materials.

Kostelnik, M. J. (Ed.) (1991). Teaching young children using themes. Glenview, IL: Scott, Foresman & Company.
> Guidelines for thematic approach to link diverse information explained. Many feasible, field-tested units adaptable to variety of substitutions described.

Leister, C. (1996). Children with Special Needs. Worthington: SRA/McGraw Hill.
> Ideas and suggestions for activities which can be adapted by a regular classroom teacher.

Wortham, S. C. (1996). The integrated classroom. Englewood Cliffs, NJ: Prentice-Hall, Inc.
> Linking assessment and curriculum to serve young children with diverse abilities and backgrounds. Prepares teachers for developmental, cultural, linguistic diversity in the classroom.

Videotapes

Bricker, D., Veltman, P., & Munkres, A. (1995). Activity-based intervention. (Video) Baltimore: Paul H. Brookes.
> Illustrates strategies to turn everyday activities and interactions into teaching and learning opportunities. Informative discussion and tips on embedding functional goals into routine, planned, and child-initiated activities.

Cripe, J. W. (1995). Family-guided activity-based intervention for infants & toddlers. (Video). Baltimore: Paul H. Brookes.
> Illustrates strategies to routine home activities and interactions into teaching and learning opportunities. Informative discussion and tips on embedding functional goals into routine, planned, and child-initiated activities.

Lindeman, D. (1996). Shining bright: Headstart inclusion. (Video) Baltimore: Paul H. Brookes.
> Interviews with teachers, administrators, and parents experiencing inclusion. Collaborative efforts and positive effects described.

Table 1.

ties in intervention, because young children have attentional constraints and many varied interests, most of their time (either individual or in groups) will be spent in play or routine activities. Play provides children the most accomodating avenue for initiating and practicing abilities in ways to improve the sophistication and elaboration of children's competencies. Routines provide support through predictability, familiarity, and repetition. Planned activities, because of the adult involvement, are excellent vehicles for acquiring new skills and generalizing emerging skills. Team members should plan together which routines or activities and the relative amount of each offers the most effective learning opportunities for children. It is important to remember this will vary according to children's interests, needs, learning style, and development. Some children will need more support from planned activities and routines. Others learn some skills such as problem solving and concept development most efficiently in play, but are uninterested in self-initiated learning of fine motor skills such as writing and drawing and need the encouragement of planned activities. There is no one perfect plan or balance of types of activities, rather planning is a dynamic process that evolves as the children learn and must be carefully monitored by their teams.

Team Planning

ABI can provide a practical framework for the team planning needed to link assessment information to children's interventions. In addition, ABI facilitates the development and implementation of individualized interventions, which are based on children's specific goals, while planning for embedding teaching and learning opportunities within child-initiated, routine and planned activities throughout the day. Children's educational teams, which include parents, can make the important decisions about how best to implement activity-based programs. Working with young children with development delays in a variety of natural environments is challenging for everyone involved. All early education, special education, and related services personnel must be willing to have open minds and be willing to implement new or modified approaches while evaluating the effectiveness of children's individualized programs. This is often easier said than done!

As a first step for any team working in inclusive settings, the members must identify children as their primary focus and be competent observers of children within early childhood environments. With a thorough understanding of children and their environments, team members can effectively plan teaching and learning opportunities related to children's individualized goals and later follow children's leads within early childhood activities to foster children's initiations (Bricker & Cripe, 1992). Focusing on children also helps the team become acquainted with one another and recognize the contributions they have made to the intervention process (Bruder, 1994).

Team work requires skills in communication, including the ability to both share and receive information. Initially, information is used to plan teaching and learning opportunities and then becomes a method for monitoring children's progress on the objectives. Team members should document children's and families' preferences and the specific strategies used to enhance learning. Documentation should prevent confusion or miscommunications among team members. As mentioned previously, inclusion often results in having additional team members who either work directly with children or provide consultation or resource information to the teachers and family members. Planning for who does what and when each activity is completed is essential to ensure an effective program for children. This also reduces the amount of redundant or conflicting questioning and increases the likelihood that supportive activities are completed in a timely manner. While often perceived as time consuming, team communication, both face-to-face and in writing, is essential for effective intervention. Mary Catherine's team meeting illustrates the importance of working together.

It's Friday morning and as Chris, Mary Catherine's dad, drops her off for the day, he joins Stephanie, Mary Catherine's teacher, Tom, her speech language pathologist, and Bonnie, the early childhood special education teacher/consultant, for a quick team meeting to discuss her progress and to make plans for the next month. (Tom and Bonnie have organized their schedules to be there early on Fridays when the children with developmental delays are dropped off so they can visit with the family members.)

Chris starts the meeting by asking about Mary Catherine's progress in eating and holding her cup. There has been concern about her slow weight gain, and the team wants to be sure that her efforts to hold and drink from her cup independently aren't further reducing her caloric intake. Tom reports about her intake during breakfast and snack, and Stephanie discusses lunch time intake. Chris suggests that they try offering Pediasure for lunch since she prefers water to juice. She drinks it at home, and it provides additional calories and nutrients that she needs. Tom and Stephanie agree it is a great idea, and Chris volunteers to bring it each day in her bag.

Stephanie tells the team that the theme for next week is "Transportation." The team begins to brainstorm ideas for Mary Catherine to participate. Tom identifies the pictures needed for her choice board, and Stephanie asks Chris if he can come on the field trip to the airport. Bonnie suggests having the children take turns riding in Mary Catherine's wheel chair as a form of transportation too. Times and opportunities for practicing her objectives are discussed for both the center and home.

Conclusion

Many children with developmental delays who participate in inclusive early childhood programs will need support to maximize their teaching and learning opportunities. Activity-based intervention provides a practical framework for children's educational teams to embed functional skill development through play and daily routines typical of high-quality, early childhood programs. Incorporating teaching and learning opportunities throughout children's day within authentic activities increases the likelihood children will acquire their individualized goals and objectives. Using an ABI approach fosters and enhances team members' ability to identify, plan, and implement intervention strategies that meet children's individualized learning needs. Through careful planning, team members can support children's individualized program within the context of an inclusive environment.

Portions of this work were supported with funding from the U.S. Department of Education, Early Education Program for Children with Disabilities, Circle of Inclusion Outreach Training Grant #HO24D40026 to the University of Kansas and from the U.S. Department of Education, Division of Personnel Preparation, Training a Collaborative Team for Infant and Toddler Community Services (TaCTICS) Grant #HO29Q50045.

References

Bailey, D. (1996). Evaluating the effectiveness of curriculum alternatives for infants and preschoolers at high risk. In M. Guralnick (Ed.), *The effectiveness of early intervention.* (pp. 227-248). Baltimore: Paul H. Brookes.

Bredekamp, S. (1987). *Developmentally appropriate practice in early childhood programs serving children from birth through age 8.* Washington, DC: National Association for the Education of Young Children.

Bricker, D., & Cripe, J. (1992). *An activity-based approach to early intervention.* Baltimore: Paul H. Brookes.

Bruder, M. B. (1994). Working with members of other disciplines: Collaboration for success. In M. Wolery & J. S. Wilbers (Eds.), *Including children with special needs in early childhood programs* (pp. 45-69). Washington, DC: National Asociation of the Education of Young Children.

Bruder, M. B. (1996). The effectiveness of specific educational/developmental curricula for children with established disabilities. In M. Guralnick (Ed.), *The effectivenes of early intervention.* (pp. 523-548). Baltimore: Paul H. Brookes.

Cook, R. E., Tessier, A., & Klein, M. D. (1996). *Adapting early childhood curricula for children in inclusive settings.* (Fourth Edition.). Columbus OH: Merrill.

Fewell, R. R., & Vadasy, P. F. (1983). *Learning through play.* Allen, TX: Development Learning Materials.

Garvey, C. (1977). *Play.* Cambridge, MA: Harvard University Press.

Koralek, D. G., Colker, L. J., & Dodge, D. T. (1993). *The what, why, and how of high-quality early childhood education: A guide for on-site supervision.* Washington, DC: National Association for the Education of Young Children.

Kostelnik, M. J., Soderman, A. K., & Whiren, A. P. (1993). *Developmentally appropriate programs in early childhood education.* New York: Macmillan Publishing.

Leister, C. (1996). *Children with Special Needs.* Worthington: SRA/McGraw Hill.

Noonan, M. J., & McCormick, L. (1993). *Early intervention in natural environments: Methods and procedures.* Pacific Grove, CA: Brooks/Cole Publishing.

Odom, S. L., & McEvoy, M. A. (1988). Integration of young children with handicaps and normally developing children. In S. L. Odom & M. B. Karnes (Eds.), *Early intervention for infants & children with handicaps: An empirical base* (pp. 241-268). Baltimore: Paul H. Brookes.

Piaget, J. (1962). *Play, dreams, and imitation.* New York: Norton.

Rogers, C. C., & Sawyers, J. K. (1988). *Play in the lives of children.* Washington, DC: National Association for the Education of Young Children.

Smilansky, S., & Shefatya, L. (1990). *Facilitating play: A medium for promoting cognitive, socio-emotional, and academic development in young children.* Gaithersburg, MD: Psychosocial and Educational Publishers.

Vygotsky, L. S. (1962). *Thought and language.* Cambridge, MA: MIT Press.

Vygotsky, L. S. (1967). Play and its role in the mental development of the child. *Soviet Psychology, 12,* 62-76.

Wolery, M., & Sainato, D. (1996). General curriculum and intervention strategies. In S. L. Odom & M. E. McLean (Eds.), *Early intervention/early childhood special education: Recommended practices* (pp. 125-158). Austin, TX: PRO-ED.

Wolery, M. (1994). Designing inclusive environments for young children with special needs. In M. Wolery & J. S. Wilbers (Eds.), *Including children with special needs in early childhood programs.* (pp. 97-118). Washington, DC: National Association for the Education of Young Children.

Wolery, M., & Wilbers, J. S. (1994). *Including children with special needs in early childhood programs.* Washington, DC: National Association for the Education of Young Children.

CHAPTER 4

Promoting Language for Children with Developmental Delays in Inclusive Settings: Effective Strategies for Early Childhood Educators

Maureen A. Conroy
University of Florida
and
William H. Brown
University of South Carolina

"Language delays are the most prevalent within the preschool population. In fact, one out of every five children demonstrates delays in communication abilities." (Bowe, 1995)

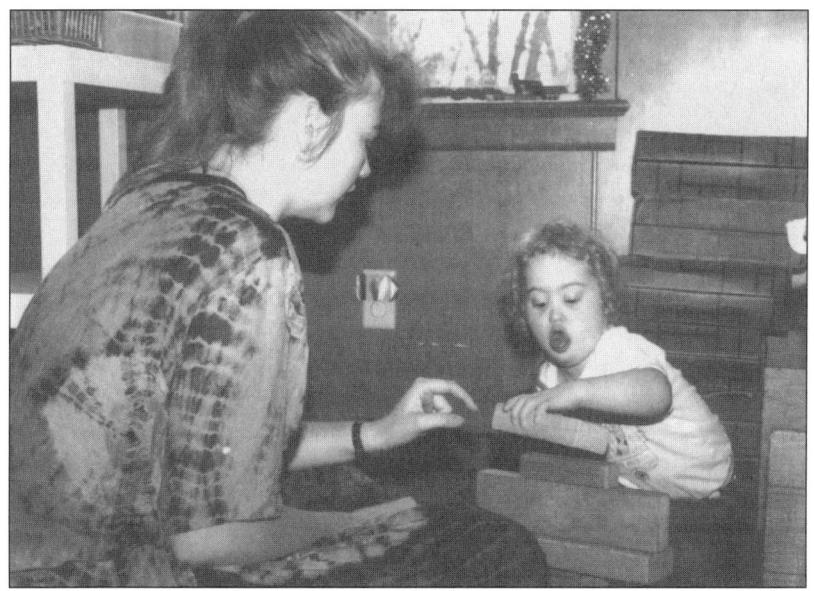

Nancy P. Alexander

During the early years, young children typically master critical developmental skills including the ability to use language. Language is a "code whereby ideas about the world are represented through a conventional system of arbitrary signals for communication" (Bloom & Lahey, 1978, p.4). Language is an essential component in the development of young children's learning and thought processes (Peterson, 1987). Through the acquisition of language, children are able to effectively interact socially, express ideas, and indicate their thoughts and desires. In addition, language provides a vehicle for thinking, processing, and organizing information and is closely linked to the development of cognitive skills (Peterson, 1987) and social skills (Guralrick, 1992).

An Overview of Language Development

Many internal and external factors affect a child's development of language. In order to develop language skills, children need to have both the physical capabilities (e.g., oral-motor abilities, sensory capabilities and processing abilities) and a supportive environment that is responsive to their communication attempts from birth (Peterson, 1987; Hart & Risley, 1992). By age five or six, most children have developed the ability to understand the meaning of words and apply grammatical structures to express their thoughts to others.

Language development involves the mastery of three critical dimensions: receptive language, expressive language, and pragmatics. Although all three of these dimensions begin developing from birth, receptive language develops more rapidly than expressive language and pragmatics. That is, young children are typically able to understand other people's language prior to being able to verbally use their own language for communication. Infants understand simple words, names, and concepts such as "bye, bye" or "ma, ma" (Bowe, 1995). By the age of two most children can understand more than 200 words. When children reach age three, they recognize names and pictures of most common objects and understand at least 500 words (Cook, Tessier, & Klein, 1996).

Expressive language develops naturally as children are able to understand the names and meanings of objects, events, and processes in their environment. Although during the first year infants are not using spoken language (i.e., adult forms), they do communicate their needs and wants. For example, an infant will cry in order to gain attention or indicate hunger. During the second year of development, receptive language dominates language development; however, children acquire the ability to combine receptive and expressive language skills to include subjects, verbs, and objects to express themselves (Bowe, 1985). Eventually children are able to express thoughts about objects, events, and processes through more advanced, complex expressive language skills. As they develop, their ability to use expressive language increases and they use combinations of words and grammatical structures to express themselves. For example, many children use simple action-object (e.g., push car) combinations as toddlers which later in development may form into more complex sentence structures (e.g., push my car, please).

The development of language not only entails the ability to understand and use expressive language, it also requires the mastery of *pragmatics*. Pragmatics is the ability of children to use language functionally and appropriately (i.e., socially) in a variety of settings (Bloom & Lahey, 1978). That is, the ability for children to understand and respond appropriately to another person's language and to communicate effectively within social situations. Pragmatics includes the use of both verbal and nonverbal skills. Examples of pragmatic skills include "taking turns" while talking, looking at the other person while conversing, and using appropriate facial gestures depending on the context of the conversation. Children initially begin to learn the social rules of language during infancy through such actions as vocalizing to gain adult attention. Eventually, they learn and master more advance social contexts and usage of language (e.g., participating in a conversation).

The development of these language dimensions (e.g., receptive, expressive, and pragmatics) are necessary for children to master and advance their language abilities and related areas of development (e.g., cognitive abilities, social competence). The mastery of each component of language enables children to become active participants in their environment (cf. Vygotsky, 1978). For example, in a preschool classroom, a teacher is conducting a "morning circle" activity. In order for the children to be full participants in the activity, they must demonstrate abilities in all languages areas (i.e., receptive, expressive, and pragmatic skills). First, they must be able to understand what the teacher is talking about in order to engage in the activity. Next, they must be able to expressively communicate their ideas to be active participants in the activity. Finally, they must be able to understand and respond appropriately to the social rules of the activity (e.g., taking turns and refraining from interrupting others). These three critical language processes enable children to fully engage in preschool activities. Moreover, language development facilitates and supports children's acquisition of other critical competencies.

How Language Delays Affect Children's Development

Language delays are the most prevalent within the preschool population. In fact, one out of every five children demonstrates delays in communication abilities (Bowe, 1995). The acquisition of language typically develops in a predictable development sequence, however, the quality and quantity of individual development varies among children (Peterson, 1987). Language delays may be a result of many variables including culture, experiences, environment, and physical-organic disabilities (Dumtschin, 1988; Peterson, 1987). Regardless of the cause of language delays in young children, these delays can seriously impact the future development of these children in a number of ways (for a review of types of language disorders see Bloom & Lahey, 1978). First, delays in language acquisition may limit children's ability to understand language used by others and may prevent them from learning new concepts (Dumtschin, 1988). In addition, language delays can negatively impact children's social interactions with peers, because they may be unable to engage in reciprocal interactions. Moreover, children with language delays may isolate themselves due to their inability to communicate effectively (Dolinar, Boser, & Holm, 1994; Duntschin, 1988). Delays in language limit children's abilities to communicate needs, wants, and ideas which in turn affect children's learning and performance in related developmental areas. Finally, language delays may cause inappropriate behavior because children become frustrated by their inability to comprehend or communicate with others. If children are unable to effectively communicate their wants, adults may not respond appropriately and their attempts to communicate will fail. This type of interaction pattern can negatively affect children's initiations and use of language. Unfortunately, children's languages difficulties may extinguish appropriate communication and exacerbate the use of tantrums and inappropriate behaviors (Peterson, 1987).

Because the development of language is a fundamental component of development and many young children demonstrate delays in language development, it is important for early childhood educators to become familiar and competent in using strategies to foster and support young children's language. The remainder of this chapter will focus on targeting language skills for instruction and using effective strategies to teach these skills in early childhood programs.

Targeting Language for Intervention: What to Teach?

Prior to designing interventions for fostering language in young children, teachers need to identify specific language skills to target for instruction. Language has three skill areas: semantic content (i.e., meaning); pragmatics (i.e., social use), and grammatical form (i.e., syntax). All three skill areas are critical for the development of language (Lahey, 1988). For example, a child who asks the teacher "Can I have more juice?" is using all three skills. The content of this example is "juice." The pragmatic function of the child's language is requesting to obtain more juice. The form of the child's language is a five-word sentence in the form of a question. Because all three skills are a critical part of the complex process of language development, teachers should target them when designing intervention strategies. Examples of specific language skills are displayed in Table 1 and a brief description of each component follows.

Content. The content of language refers to the meaning or semantics of language. Children learn the meaning of words through their experiences and interactions with their environment. For example, a child picks up a round rubber toy that bounces and begins to examine it. The child's father responds to his actions by saying "It's a ball." The child begins to associate the word "ball" with round rubber objects. After repeated exposure to round rubber objects, the child begins to learn and generalize the concept of "ball." Through this active engagement with and naming of objects, children begin to develop meanings for words, actions, and objects in their environment. Additionally, children begin to learn the meaning of semantic relations (Bloom & Lahey, 1978). Semantic relations provide meaning for the interaction and relationship between various actions, objects, and persons. For example, children learn the concept of "recurrence," "disappearance," or "appearance" in relation to different objects and persons. A child may request "more cookie," acknowledge the disappearance of her mother (e.g., "no mommy"), or acknowledge the appearance of an object (e.g., that ball). Children also demonstrate the semantic relations of rejection (e.g., "no bath"), actions in relation to people and object (e.g., "up Daddy"), location of objects or someone such as "Mommy car,"

Developmental Age	Semantics	Phonology/Syntax	Pragmatics
1 - 6 months	Begins to recognize names of objects and people	Vocalizes sounds (e.g., cooing/babbling)	Looks and responds to speaker by vocalizing
6 - 12 months	Increases recognition of names of common objects and people	Combines consonant and vowel sounds (e.g., mama, dada, baba)	"Takes turns" when someone is speaking
12 - 18 months	Points to familiar objects and people Begins to demonstrate understanding of semantic relational words, (e.g., more)	Says one word utterances consisting of nouns and verbs (e.g., ball, more)	Follows one-two step directions
18 - 24 months	Increases understanding of semantic relational words (e.g., all gone)	Combines two words together (e.g., mommy go, big doggie)	Uses "speech" to gain attention
24 - 28 months	Increases understanding of nouns, verbs, adjectives, and adverbs	Uses short phrases Asks questions (e.g., where Daddy go?)	Uses "speech" to request items, protest, comment, greet, and answer questions
28 - 36 months	Identifies names and pictures of most common objects	Uses possessives (e.g., my), articles (e.g., an, a), plurals, and some prepositions	Uses "speech" to obtain demands and control
36 - 42 months	Increases receptive vocabulary skills including pronouns	Uses simple sentences Uses pronouns Includes endings on words	Uses "speech" for social control, asks questions
42 - 48 months	Increases receptive vocabulary of nouns verbs, adjectives, adverbs, prepositions, pronouns, etc.	Uses a variety of sentence structures including adjectives Coordinates use of simple sentences	Sustains topics; begins role playing
48 - 60 months	Develops a receptive vocabulary of over 500 words	Uses pronouns and verb tenses accurately	Engages in conversational skills

Adapted from the following sources: Bloom & Lahey, 1978; Brown, 1973, Cook, Tessier, & Klein, 1996; Noonan & McCormick, 1993; Peterson, 1987)

Table 1. Sample Language Skills to Target for Instruction

possession (e.g., "ball mine"), and descriptors including adverbs and adjectives (e.g., "stove hot"). Children's language content progresses over time beginning with the recognition of several common objects and people during infancy to a sophisticated vocabulary of over 500 words by the age of three.

Pragmatics. As described previously, pragmatics refers to the social functions in which language is used to communicate with others across a variety of situations. A particular setting, the persons involved, the content and topic of the conversation, the goal of the conversation, the times and place of the conversation, and many other factors may determine the pragmatic function of the conversations (Hooper & Naremore, 1978). For example, children learn to recognize and respond appropriately to facial cues (e.g., a frown or head shake) given by adults when they want the children not to interrupt an ongoing conversation. In addition, children learn through early interactions with their parents to "take turns" in a conversation. Many parents will indirectly teach children this skill by imitating a young infant "cooing" and respond by "cooing" back and forth in a turn taking manner. Pragmatic skills demonstrated in early childhood include the following functions:

➡ requesting attention (e.g., saying "look");

➡ requesting a want or desire (e.g., saying "I want more milk");

➡ protesting (e.g., saying "no");

➡ commenting (e.g., saying "big dog");

➡ greeting (e.g., saying "bye, bye"); and

➡ answering questions (e.g., saying "my ball) (Noonan & McCormick, 1993).

As you can see these pragmatic skills are closely linked with the content skills described above, but also serve a specific function. As children's pragmatic skills develop, they are able to participate appropriately in variety of complex conversations using verbal and nonverbal cues.

Form. The form of language includes both syntax and morphology. Syntax refers to the correct word order used in sentences. Morphology refers to the grammatical structure of individual words. Knowing how to combine words into sentences and using correct grammatical structure are critical skills to target for intervention. Often these skills are learned through adult-child and child-child interaction and the observation of appropriate language models. In addition, feedback is often provided as children learn and experiment with their own form of language. Infants begin to learn this language dimension through the initial vocalizations of syllables followed by babbling and jargon. As children's language develops, they begin to formulate consonant and vowel combinations into intelligible words. When their form becomes more complex, they are able to combine the use of nouns, verbs, pronouns, adjectives, and relational words into sentences to express meaning. Once again, the form of children's language is related to their ability to use and understand language.

These brief descriptions of the different language dimensions outline specific skills and areas that should be targeted for language intervention. Prior to determining language goals for a specific child, a comprehensive assessment and evaluation of that child's language and cognitive abilities should be conducted by qualified professionals which may include speech-language pathologists, early interventionists, health related professionals, and occupational and physical therapists. These professionals have the expertise to determine the nature of the language delay or disorder and to assist the teacher in targeting appropriate goals and designing intervention strategies to meet the unique language needs and abilities of the child. The assessment should include a comprehensive sampling of the child's language skills including form, function, and content (see Goldstein, Kaczmarek, & Hepting, 1996 for a review of recommended assessment guidelines). With the expertise and collaborative consultation of trained professionals, an early childhood educator can become the primary language interventionist for the children with language delays (Cole, Dale, & Mills, 1991).

Language goals should be targeted at the level at which the child is presently using language. The teacher will want to accept the child's language level and expand on one or more skill area (i.e., form, function, or use) (Dolinar, et al., 1994). As Prizant and Bailey (1992) suggested, the focus of intervention should be not only on increasing the child's vocabulary, but expanding the child's syntax and use of language including expanding the functions and ability to analyze language input and structures, teaching persistence at using language, and developing conversational skills. For example, for a child who is speaking in one word utterance an appropriate language goal may be to teach the child to use two-three word utterances to facilitate his asking for needs and wants. An example of this sequence can be seen in Table 2.

As illustrated above, learning two-three word utterances includes instruction in all three skill areas of language; that is, content, form, and pragmatics. Regardless of the language skills targeted for instruction, it is important that the skills enable children to communicate functionally and effectively with others in their environment.

Teaching Language Skills

Language is an integral part of children's day and teaching language should take place within the natural contexts in which it occurs with familiar peers and adults (Prizant & Bailey, 1992). The natural environment is where most children learn language which makes it an ideal setting for intervention. When specific language skills are taught in the natural environment, they are functional, generalization occurs across people and settings, and a normal context is provided

	Content	Form	Use
Existing Language Skills	Demonstrates understanding of common nouns, verbs, and semantic relations	Uses two word utterances including nouns and verbs (e.g., more banana)	Request attention and comment
Tarketed Language Skills	Increase vocabulary ot include pronouns	Uses two-three word utterances including pronouns (e.g., help me please)	Ask for assistance

Table 2. Planning Language Intervention Targets

(Yoder et al., 1995). As children encounter language interactions within the day, such as relating information regarding needs, knowledge, feelings, and ideas; these interactions can be used to teach specific language skills. Intervention should occur frequently throughout the day and emphasize the functional use of language skills. Functional use of language consist of those language interventions that will enable the child to interact with his or her environment effectively. No single intervention technique is the "best." Teachers should be knowledgeable about and be able to use multiple approaches to address the unique needs of each child. Although many teachers may need consultation support from other professionals on goal selection and intervention strategies, it is appropriate for the classroom teacher to be the primary language interventionist while the child is at school (Cole et al., 1990).

Throughout daily contacts that occur naturally, teachers can make a significant impact on a children's language development. Dumtschin (1988) outlined several factors teachers should consider during these "teachable moments." First, teachers should frequently converse with all children in the classroom even if they are nonverbal. Frequent, ongoing conversations about objects and events that are familiar to children can help support their language development. When talking with a specific child, teachers should match and expand on the child's language abilities. The adults in the classroom need to "listen and respond" appropriately when a child uses language. A responsive environment where language focuses on the children's interests is critical. Teachers should remember to encourage children to initiate interactions and use language to obtain information and address needs (Cook et al., 1996). Children need to learn how to actively engage others in conversation (e.g., asking questions). Although teachers should provide general, conversational support, they should also encourage children to use spontaneous imitation of new words and forms not just responses to questions (Jones & Warren, 1991).

Sometimes an enriched, responsive environment may not provide enough direct support for facilitating all children's language development. There are a variety of naturalistic intervention strategies that can be used to teach children language. When teachers use naturalistic strategies, instruction occurs in a careful and well-planned manner, but is not intrusive to the children and their classrooms (Noonan & McCormick, 1993). When using naturalistic strategies, "the environment is altered to increase the probability that the desired behavior will occur" (Noonan & McCormick, 1993, p.238). In the case of language intervention, the topic of language is usually initiated by a child and results in a natural consequence for the child (e.g., if the child wants and asks for juice, the child is given juice). Teacher input is relatively brief and occurs naturally throughout the day (Noonan & McCormick, 1993). The following are brief descriptions of several naturalistic intervention strategies that can be used by early childhood educators to promote children's language. When using these intervention strategies, teachers should begin with the "least intrusive" strategy (e.g., environmental arrangement) prior to moving to more structured approaches (e.g., incidental teaching) as may be indicated by the needs and language level of the child.

Environmental Arrangement for Facilitating Language

Children's environments play a critical role in facilitating language skills (Hart & Risely, 1992). To support children's use of language, teachers should arrange their classroom environments so they provide many physical and social opportunities for children to use language. Classroom environments with many interesting toys and materials will motivate children to use their language. Often, teachers forget that they can alter the classroom environment and that children's behavior can change with "less" direct effort (Bailey & Wolery, 1992). Cook and her colleagues (1996) suggested several strategies teachers can use that will facilitate the use of language skills. These strategies include:

➡ Providing choices for children to encourage them to indicate needs and wants;

➡ Providing opportunities for children to initiate or respond prior to "jumping in" and "filling in the blanks";

➡ Attending to children's use of language immediately;

➡ Encouraging children to find out information, request help, obtain attention, and comment using language; and

➡ Encouraging social interactions between children and peers.

Different environmental factors to consider when designing a language enriched environment are:
- the types of materials in the classroom
- the schedule
- the organization and structure of instructional activities
- the peers and adults in the classroom (Bailey & Wolery, 1992).

Types of materials. Materials in the environment should be physically responsive and encourage active exploration so that children have objects and activities to talk about. Materials should be novel, but within children's knowledge base so that exploration is encouraged. Noonan and McCormick (1993) suggested that teachers categorize materials according to their complexity and developmental levels dividing the toys and materials into different sets which contain a variety of different levels. Teachers should rotate toys and materials regularly to retain the novelty effect and encourage exploration. As Jones and Warren (1991) described, teachers will want to provide moderate novelty, that is, embedding new objects in a familiar routine. As children actively engage and explore their classroom environment, many language skills will emerge. Children's frequent engagement with materials will facilitate and support their language acquisition.

The following is an example the effects of novelty may have on a child's language.

> Marcus is a four year old with developmental language delays. Although he can use several word utterances to communicate, he rarely initiates interactions. During "center time," Marcus enjoys "cooking and cleaning" in the housekeeping area. Marcus' teacher, Ms. Karen, continually rotates toys and materials. Today, she has placed different toy food items in the housekeeping area. When Marcus enters the housekeeping area, he immediately notices the new toys and says excitedly "Look what we got." Marcus' verbal initiation provides the vehicle for Ms. Karen to respond and discuss with Marcus the different types of new food in the housekeeping area.

Schedule. One way children learn language is through the use of predictable routines (Noonan & McCormick, 1993). Through a well-sequenced schedule children will learn word meanings, use of language, and observe different forms of language. A daily schedule can help children develop concepts about their school day, activities, and people including the sequencing of events or activities, peers and adult's names, meanings of words, semantic relations, and pragmatic skills. The importance of a schedule is illustrated in the following example.

> Mr. Cole, a Head Start teacher, has outlined a schedule for the children in his class to follow each day. After arriving a school, the first activity on Mr. Cole's schedule is a morning circle. During morning circle, Mr. Cole reviews the schedule with his students. They vocalize and learn the sequence of activities during the day, concepts about what activities happen "first," "next," "before," and "after," and plan what they will do during the day. The students learn the names of activities, who is involved in the activity, and where the activities are located. As they follow the daily schedule, the names, locations, and activities are reinforced and used by the students.

Once a predictable sequence of events has been established, interrupting a schedule, routine, or withholding or delaying an expected event can also encourage language (Noonan & McCormick, 1993). For example, if children are expecting to have "story time" prior to rest period, teachers may want to pretend to skip the story time "by mistake" one day. Teacher's "mistakes" may provoke children's language about the change in the daily schedule. Children may enjoy reminding adults about "rules."

Organization and structure of activities. The activities in the classroom should cover a broad area of different levels, learning styles, and language abilities of the children (Bailey & Wolery, 1992; Prizant & Bailey, 1992). Language instruction should occur during group activities so that children have an opportunity to observe and imitate appropriate peer language abilities. All areas of the classroom should be carefully designed to support children's use of language. For example, the socio-dramatic play area where a great deal of social interaction occurs can be used to teach social aspects of language. Arts and crafts are a good activity to use to teach specific language skills such as prepositions, forms, nouns, and spatial relations. The reading and language arts center encourages language content development through the use of pictures, puppets, books, and writing materials. Finally, mealtimes are an excellent activity for teaching children conversational skills, taking turns, requesting needs and wants, and fostering conceptual development. Activities can be planned that will facilitate the specific language skills needed to be taught to individual children within the context of the classroom (for further information on using activity-based teaching, see Chapter 3 of this book). The use of activities designed to teach specific language skills is outlined in the following example.

> Cadena is a young child with severe expressive language delays enrolled in an inclusive early childhood program. One specific language skill which has been targeted for Cadena is to learn to say the word "more" to indicate her needs and wants. The classroom teacher has designed several activities during the day that will help teach Cadena to use "more" to request food, materials or activity.

During outside play Cadena enjoys sitting on a swing and being pushed by the teacher. Occasionally the teacher will intentionally stop pushing Cadena and encourage her to use the word "more" to indicate she wants to be pushed again. In addition, during snack, the teacher will ask the class if anyone would like more juice. She will encourage Cadena to use the word "more" to indicate she wants more juice.

Peer and adult language models in the classroom. Another important component of environmental language intervention is having appropriate language models available (Dolinar, et al., 1994). Peers and adults can be excellent intervention tools by modeling appropriate language. Adults can facilitate language in young children by engaging them in frequent conversation that match the child's age level, asking questions, and allowing the child to "speak," regardless of their form, expanding on their conversational skills (Dumtschin, 1988). Language models should speak slowly and distinctly, keep sentences short, talk about the "here and now," use words that can easily be understood, and listen attentively to the target child (Cook et al., 1996). It is important to have peers in the classroom who provide appropriate use of language skills in addition to appropriate form and content (Prizant & Bailey, 1992). Young children will often imitate their peer's language during activities as explained below.

Ms. Beverly is making pudding with the class. A small group of children is seated around the table with Ms. Beverly. Kevin, a young child with language delays is part of the small group. Ms. Beverly asks "who wants to stir the pudding?" Alison quickly says "I want to." Ms. Beverly passes the bowl to Alison. Alison stirs the pudding several times and Ms. Beverly asks "who wants to stir the pudding?" Having observed Alison's behavior, Kevin models Alison's language and says "I want to." Ms. Beverly passes him the bowl.

Instructional Teaching Strategies

An appropriate language environment fosters language development in many young children, however, due to a specific child's delays, a teacher may need to implement a more individualized approach combining environmental arrangement and specific teaching strategies to facilitate language. The following are descriptions of specific intervention strategies that involve more direct assistance and contact from the teacher. The focus of the teaching interaction is still child-initiated and directed, however.

Incidental Teaching. Incidental teaching is one of the most widely used naturalistic teaching techniques (Noonan & McCormick, 1993) and has been used effectively with children to increase their language skills (for reviews see Hart & Risely, 1974, 1975, 1980; Kaiser et al., 1992; Warren & Gazdag, 1990). According to Warren and Kaiser (1986) incidental teaching involves:

➡ arranging the environment to increase the likelihood that the child will initiate an interaction;

➡ selecting language targets appropriate to the child's individual level, interest, and opportunities and facilitating engagement;

➡ intervening and responding to the child's initiation with a request for a more complex language form through prompting; and

➡ reinforcing the child's language efforts by providing attention and access to the desired objects or events. This is illustrated in the example below.

Ms. Holly's class is planting flowers in their outdoor garden. The class is grouped around Ms. Holly as she digs a hole for her flower. She explains to the class that they will need to dig their own holes in order to plant their flowers. Ms. Holly hands the shovel to Ben. Ben's language goal is to spontaneously use two word utterances. Ben tries to dig his hole, but is unable to do it independently. He turns to Ms. Holly and says "help." Ms. Holly says "help with what?" Ben answers " help dig." Ms. Holly says "Yes, I'll help you dig" and provides the assistance requested.

Mand-model. Teachers may need to use verbal prompts to encourage children to use and expand their language skills. These include task directions, questions, requests, and models (Noonan & McCormick, 1993). This approach is a good technique to use for children who do not initiate (Jones & Warren, 1991). The following is an example of a teacher implementing mand-model strategies.

Jose is in the block area of the classroom. The teacher notices that Jose is trying to reach a basket of Legos that are out of reach. She asks him, "Jose, what do you want?" Jose responds by pointing to the Legos. The teacher expands Jose's communication attempt and provides the verbal prompt "Tell me what those are." Jose responds by pointing and whining. The teacher provides a model "Say Lego." Jose says "Lego." The teacher responds by repeating Jose's response "That's right, Legos" while handing him the basket of Legos.

Time delay procedures. Children with language delays will often learn to stop initiating interactions and wait for an adult or a peer to initiate to them first. A time delay procedure consists of teachers "waiting" for children to initiate prior to responding. This procedure teaches children to initiate and learn to control their environment using language. An example of a teacher using time delay procedures follows.

> Susie is eating lunch with her peers in the lunchroom. Everyone's dessert is in the center of the table. The teacher notices that Susie is looking at her dessert and looks at the teacher. The teacher waits for Susie to verbally request her dessert. Susie waits a minute and eventually asks the teacher for her dessert. The teacher responds to Susie and gives her the dessert. If Susie did not respond within a minute, the teacher could have used a verbal prompt (e.g., "Do you want something Susie?") in order to encourage her to initiate.

This section has outlined several strategies teachers can implement to facilitate language skills in young children with delays. No single strategy is the "best" to use. These strategies can be used alone or in combination. The teacher will want to consider the specific goals the child need to learn and use the strategy that can best meet those needs.

Evaluating the Effects of Intervention

In order to determine if the intervention strategies employed are successful, ongoing evaluation of the children's target goals should occur. Bailey and Wolery (1992) outlined the following strategies to use for evaluating the effectiveness of the intervention. First, teachers should identify the purpose or outcome of the intervention. That is, what changes should occur in children's language as a result of the intervention efforts. Next, periodically, teachers should observe the children's behavior in relation to the targeted language goals and intervention strategies and determine whether the targeted changes have occurred. As Schwartz and Olswang (1996) illustrated, teachers may want to develop questions that will help them determine if their goals have been met and what aspects of the intervention have helped children attain their language targets. For example, if a child's goal is to initiate requests to a peer, the teacher will want to observe the child during an unstructured free play activity to determine if she or he is initiating to peers. In addition, the teacher will want to observe which particular activities and peers the child engages with most frequently. If the goals have been met, the teacher can develop new language targets for instruction using the factors that facilitate the child's use of language. If the child's goals have not been met, the teacher will want to determine the reasons. Were there enough opportunities for the child to use language? Was the environment appropriately arranged? Did the teacher implement the required activities that facilitate language use? Were the desired outcomes met? Following a careful examination of the environmental and instructional factors, the teacher should make changes consistent with the results of the evaluation. It is critical for ongoing evaluation, adaptation, and follow-up to occur on a consistent basis in order to provide the appropriate instructional supports to facilitate a child's language.

Conclusion

This chapter has provided an overview of language development and the importance of language skills for young children. Selected language intervention targets have been reviewed and effective instructional strategies have been outlined. As described, classroom teachers play a critical role in the development of language in young children. Although most children develop language through a predictable developmental process, some children do not. These children with language delays are not only at risk for language disabilities, but are also at risk for further social and cognitive delays. The natural context for language, which occurs in children's homes and classrooms, is the best place for instruction to be implemented. Teachers can provide many teaching and learning opportunities to facilitate children's language through the careful arrangement of physical and social environmental factors. In addition to arranging the environment, teachers may need to implement other naturalistic language intervention strategies that have facilitated specific language skills in young children. Through the use of these effective strategies, teachers will observe the active use and fostering of language within their classroom.

References

Alpert, C., & Kaiser, A. P. (1992). Training parents as milieu language teachers. *Journal of Early Intervention*, 16, 31-52.

Bailey, D. B., & Wolery, M. (1992). Designing and arranging environments. In D. Bailey & M. Wolery (Eds.) *Teaching infants and preschoolers with disabilities (Second Edition)* (pp. 198-228). New York: Macmillan Publishing Company.

Bloom, L., & Lahey, M. (1978). *Language development and language disorders*. New York: John Wiley.

Bowe, F. (1985). *Birth to five: Early childhood special education*. New York: Delmar Publishers.

Brown, R. (1973). *A first language: The early stages*. Cambridge, MA: Harvard University Press.

Cole, K., Dale, P., & Mills, P. (1990). Defining language delay in young children by cognitive referencing: Are we saying more than we know? *Applied Psycholinguistics*, 11, 291-302.

Cooke, R. E., Tessier, A., & Klein, M. D. (1996). Nurturing communication skills. In R. E. Cook, A. Tessier, & M. D. Klein (Eds.), *Adapting early childhood curricula for children in inclusive settings (Fourth Edition)* (pp. 312-16). Englewood Cliffs, NJ: Merrill.

Dolinar, K., Boser, C., & Holm, E. (1994). *Learning through play: Curriculum and activities for inclusive classroom.* Albany, NY: Delmar Publisher.

Dumtschin, J. U. (1988). Recognizing language development and delay in early childhood. *Young Children*, 43, 16-24.

Goldstein, H., Kaczmarek, L. A., & Hepting, N. H. (1996). Indicators of quality communication intervention. In S. L. Odom & M. E. McLean (Eds.), *Early intervention/early childhood special education: Recommended practices* (pp. 197-221). Austin, TX: PRO-ED.

Guralnick, M. J. (1992). A hierarchical model for understanding children's peer-related social competence. In S. L. Odom, S. R. McConnell, & M. A. McEvoy (Eds.), *Social competence of young children with disabilities: Issues and strategies for intervention* (pp. 37-64). Baltimore: Paul H. Brookes.

Hart, B., & Risely, T.R. (1974). Using preschool materials to modify the language of disadvantaged children. *Journal of Applied Behavior Analysis*, 7, 243-256.

Hart, B., & Risely, T.R. (1975). Incidental teaching of language in the preschool. *Journal of Applied Behavior Analysis*, 8, 411-420.

Hart, B., & Risely, T. R. (1980). In vivo language training: Unanticipated and general effects. *Journal of Applied Behavior Analysis*, 13, 407-432.

Hart, B., & Risley, T. R (1992). American parenting of language-learning children: Persisting differences in family-child interactions observed in natural home environments. *Developmental Psychology*, 28, 1096-1105.

Hooper, R., & Naermore, R. J. (1978). *Children's speech: A practical introduction to communication development.* New York: Harper & Row.

Jones, H. A., & Warren, S. F. (1991). Enhancing engagement in early language teaching. *Teaching exceptional children*, 23, 48-50.

Kaiser, A. P., Yoder, P. J., & Keetz, A. (1992). Evaluating milieu teaching. In S.F. Warren & J. Reichle (Eds.), *Causes and effects in communication and language intervention* (Vol.1, pp.9-47). Baltimore: Paul H. Brookes.

Lahey, M. (1988). *Language disorders and language development.* Englewood Cliffs, NJ: Merrill.

Noonan, M. J., & McCormick, L. (1993). *Early intervention in natural environments: Methods and procedures.* Pacific Grove, CA: Brooks/Cole.

Swartz, I. S., & Olswang, L. B. (1996). Evaluating child behavior change in natural settings: Exploring alternative strategies for data collection. *Topics in Early Childhood Special Education*, 16, 82-101.

Peterson, N. L. (1987). *Early intervention for handicapped and at-risk children: An introduction to early childhood-special education.* Denver, CO: Love Publishing Company.

Prizant, B., & Bailey, D. (1992). Facilitating the acquisition and use of communication skills. In D. B. Bailey & M. Wolery (Eds.). *Teaching infants and preschoolers with disabilities (Second Edition)* (pp.299-361). New York: Macmillan Publishing Company.

Warren, S. F., & Gazdag, G. (1990). Facilitating early language development with milieu intervention procedures. *Journal of Early Intervention*, 14, 62-86.

Warren, S. F., & Kaiser, A. (1986). Incidental language teaching: A critical review. *Journal of Speech and Hearing Disoders*, 51, 291-299.

Vygotsky, L. S. (1978). *Mind in society: The development of higher psychological processes.* Cambridge, MA: Harvard University Press.

Yoder, P. J., Kaiser, A. P., Goldstein, H., Alpert, C., Mousetis, L., Kaczmarek, L., & Fischer, R. (1995). An exploratory comparison of milieu teaching and responsive interaction in the classroom applications. *Journal of Early Intervention*, 19, 218-242.

CHAPTER 5

Promoting and Supporting Peer Interactions in Inclusive Preschools: Effective Strategies for Early Childhood Educators

William H. Brown
University of South Carolina

Maureen A. Conroy
University of Florida

> *"Many educators have asserted that the acquisition of effective social behavior with adults and peers is a fundamental feature of early childhood development."*

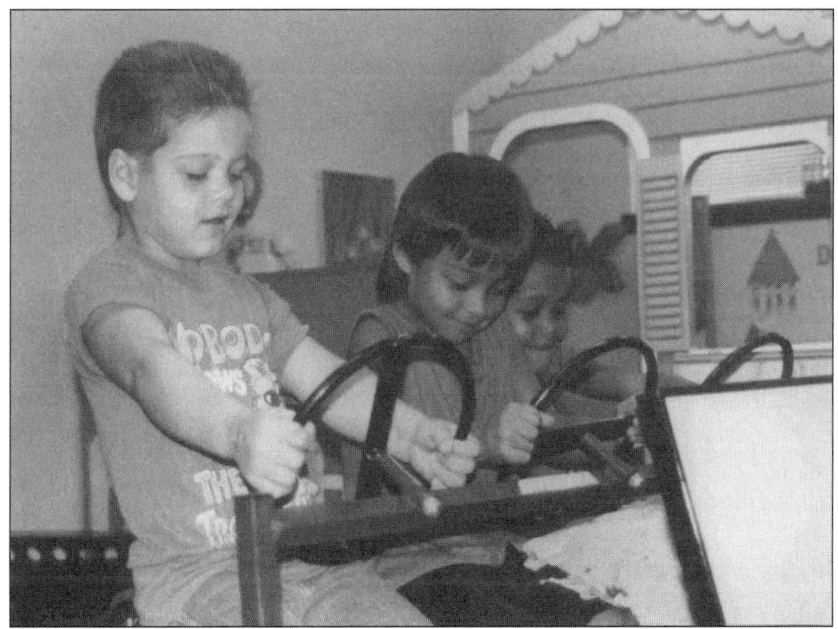

Nancy P. Alexander

Child development researchers have noted that early in life, infants become social with familiar adults such as parents and caregivers (e.g., Howes, 1987). Researchers have also reported that during the second year of life, infants and toddlers begin to interact, albeit briefly, with other young children. Sociability, or children's tendency to seek social interaction from others, has been viewed as a trait that begins to be established during the second year of life. Moreover, young children's peer interactions increase in frequency and complexity as they mature socially throughout their preschool years (see Hartup, 1992; Ladd & Coleman, 1993 for recent reviews).

Child development theorists with diverse perspectives have agreed that successful adult-child and child-child social interactions provide both a context and a mechanism for acquiring and elaborating children's essential abilities such as social, language, and cognitive competencies (cf. Bijou, 1993; Flavel, 1977; Piaget, 1926; Vygotsky, 1978). Many educators have asserted that the acquisition of effective social behavior with adults and peers is a fundamental feature of early childhood development (cf. Guralnick, 1992, 1994; Hartup, 1992; Ladd & Coleman, 1993; Odom, McConnell, & McEvoy, 1992). Specifically, young children's peer interactions have provided a rich route for acquiring a variety of developmental abilities which range from relatively simple greetings to much more complex language and pretend play. Moreover, children's emergent peer-related social competence[1] has been a critical developmental process during early childhood when peer relations and initial friendships are being formed (cf. Guralnick, 1992, 1994; Hartup, 1992; Ladd & Coleman, 1993).

In contrast to young children who are friendly and socially sophisticated, researchers have noted that young children who have peer interaction difficulties and who fail to develop positive peer relationships are at risk for behavioral difficulties and social maladjustment in later life (cf. Hartup, 1992; Parker & Asher, 1987). Indeed, Asher (1990) noted that as many as 10% of young children may have peer-related social competence problems that might result in peer rejection during early childhood and difficulties in later childhood. In particular young children with a variety of developmental difficulties have been at risk for social interaction problems during early childhood. Specifically, young children with developmental delays (e.g., Kopp, Baker, & Brown, 1992), behavioral problems (e.g., McMahon & Forehand, 1988), and histories of child abuse and neglect (e.g., Mueller & Silverman, 1989) have been identified as high risk for having difficulties in their peer interactions (cf. Brown, 1995).[2]

A general consensus about the importance of peer interactions and peer-related social competence has existed for many years in the field of early childhood. Enhancing young children's peer-related social competence has been a primary goal for many parents and professionals during early childhood (cf. Mize, 1995). Because of the critical nature of young children's peer-related social competence, many early childhood educators have advocated the explicit inclusion of peer interaction interventions in early childhood programs, particularly those programs that serve children who are at risk for social competence problems (e.g., Brown & Odom, 1995; Guralnick, 1994; McEvoy & Odom, 1996; Mize, 1995; Odom & Brown, 1993). In addition, memberships of professional organizations [e.g., National Association for the Education of Young Children (Bredekamp, 1987; Bredekamp & Rosegrant, 1992; NAEYC & NAESC/SDE, 1991); Division of Early Childhood of the Council for Exceptional Children (DEC Task Force on Recommended Practices, 1993)], have endorsed the integration of social competence activities into contemporary preschool curricula.

Identification of Preschool Children with Peer Interaction Problems

Given the importance of preschool children's peer interactions, early childhood educators need to be able to identify those children who have peer-related social competence difficulties. Traditionally, four methods have been used to identify young children who are having social development difficulties:

➡ teacher nominations (i.e., selecting those children teachers believe are withdrawn or have disruptive patterns of peer interactions);

➡ direct observation of children's peer interactions;

➡ sociometric assessment; and

➡ standardized assessment with behavioral rating scales (see Brown, Odom, & Holcombe, 1996 for discussion of assessment of social behavior).

Although many social competence researchers have recommended multimethod, multi-source, and multi-setting procedures to obtain comprehensive assessments of young children's peer-related social competence, that approach has been very labor intensive and probably unnecessary except for well-specified research or clinical purposes (cf. Brown et al., 1996). We have suggested a relatively straightforward process for identifying young children who might benefit from peer-related social competence activities (Brown, Ragland, & Bishop, 1989a). First and foremost, an understanding of "normal social development" has been beneficial for teachers who are interested in identifying young children with peer-related social difficulties and improving their peer-related social competence. In general, preschool children's normal social development has been characterized by:

- interacting positively and frequently with adults and peers
- sharing materials, time, and space
- respecting the property of others
- acquiring a conscience (i.e., learning basic social rules and behaving appropriately in a variety of social situations)
- understanding feelings of self, peers, and others
- having positive self-concept and sense of self-worth.[3]

Given an understanding of preschool children's social development, we have recommended that teachers, who are familiar with child development in general and the behavior of the preschool children in their programs in particular, nominate those children who they believe have peer-related social competence difficulties. Specifically, teachers should select those children who appear socially isolated by identifying children who are the least verbal and who rarely interact with peers. Following teacher nominations, to verify their selections, we have asked teachers to observe the children they nominated as needing improvement in their peer-related social competence. Specifically, we have recommended teachers observe children systematically in preschool settings where peer interactions occur frequently (e.g., activity centers, indoor and outdoor free play). Several teacher observations have been helpful in verifying whether children have peer interaction difficulties. In addition, teachers have developed a better understanding of the observed children's individual needs. Through careful observation of play activities, teachers have been able to identify children who are:

- socially withdrawn or sociable
- mature or immature
- dependent or independent
- helpful or domineering
- aggressive or assertive.

Potential Warning Signs of Social Competence Problems in Preschool Children

1. <u>Separation problems</u>. Children who are older than three years of age and who have persistent and severe difficulty when separating from their parents or other familiar adults may be overdependent on adults. Children's over dependence on adults may inhibit their exploration of the learning environment and peer interactions.

2. <u>Social withdrawal</u>. Children with frequent and persistent "shyness" may have social development problems. Particularly if their withdrawal prevents them from taking part in routine activities. With some children, a chronic pattern of withdrawal may severely inhibit their interactions with peers and the formation of friendships.

3. <u>Attention and overactivity problems</u>. Children who are overactive and frequently change from one activity to another may be at risk for social development problems. Because these children are changing activities often, they miss many learning opportunities and do not experience sustained social interactions with peers. The lack of sustained social interaction with peers may inhibit the establishment and maintenance of positive peer relationships.

4. <u>Noncompliance with teacher requests or classroom rules</u>. Children who consistently fail to comply with teacher instructions or who do not follow well-established classroom rules may be oppositional or noncompliant. They may not participate as often or as well as other children in classroom activities, particularly in classroom games that have rules. Noncompliance and a lack of participation may inhibit their development of cooperative behavior and respect for others.

5. <u>Language and cognitive delays</u>. Children who have language or cognitive delays may have difficulties in various social interactions. Because preschool children's social interactions with peers become more verbal as they mature, children with cognitive and language delays may be excluded from many social situations. They may become less likely to initiate interactions and less responsive to their peers' initiations.

6. <u>Aggression and tantrums</u>. Children who are overly aggressive or tantrum frequently and who grab toys and materials from others and will not share will probably have fewer positive social interactions with peers and may have difficulties in forming friendships.

7. <u>Excessive attention seeking</u>. Children who make excessive demands on adults by frequently whining, crying, or asking to be helped or to be held may have difficulties interacting with other children. If children are overly adult-centered in their interactions, they may not develop positive peer relationships.

Table 1.

The seven potential warning signs of social competence problems delineated in Table 1 should assist preschool teachers in identifying young children who may need additional support and encouragement in their social development. A relatively simple and straightforward process of teachers first selecting children who may have difficulties, and then verifying through direct observation whether the selected children have peer interaction difficulties during common preschool activities, has been a reasonable and effective approach for identify young with peer-related social competence problems (cf. Brown et al., 1989a; Greenwood, Walker, Todd, & Hops, 1979). For a small number of young children who have severe and persistent peer-interaction or behavioral problems (e.g., chronic and dangerous aggressive behavior, incidents of property destruction, frequent noncompliance) across several months, teachers may need to consult with professionals who have worked with children with significant behavioral difficulties (e.g., special educators, psychologists) and pursue further assessment (cf. Campbell, 1990; Merrell, 1994).

Identification of Critical Peer Interaction Competencies for Preschool Children

After teachers have identified children who might benefit from peer interaction interventions, they are faced with "what to teach" (cf. Conroy, Langenbrunner, & Burleson, 1996; Tremblay, Strain, Hendrickson, & Shores, 1981). Researchers have determined "what to teach" by using two basic approaches: asking teachers to rate and report peer-related social competence skills that "successful" children employ (e.g., Kostelnik, Soderman, & Whiren, 1993; Noonan et al., 1992); and, directly observing children's social interactions to determine "successful" social behavior (e.g., Conroy & Fox, 1995; Tremblay et al., 1981).

These two lines of inquiry have yielded several critical peer-related behavioral competencies that are appropriate to promote and support during peer interaction activities and peer interaction interventions. The 13 critical peer-related social competencies delineated in Table 2 should assist preschool teachers in identifying "what to teach" when working with young children who may need additional support and encouragement to improve their peer interactions.

A Hierarchy for Promoting and Supporting Preschool Children's Peer Interactions

After early childhood educators have become familiar with young children's critical peer-related social competencies and they have determined which children might benefit from peer-related social competence activities, we have recommended that teachers employ a decision-making hierarchy to determine intervention strategies that might improve young children's peer interactions, their peer-related social competence, and ultimately, their peer relationships (see Figure 1 entitled Strategies for Promoting and Supporting Preschool Children's Peer Interactions).[4] Our purpose for developing the decision-making hierarchy has been to assist educators in planning and selecting interventions that are both compatible with (i.e., interventions teachers have used in their classrooms) and effective in preschool settings (i.e., validated by applied research).

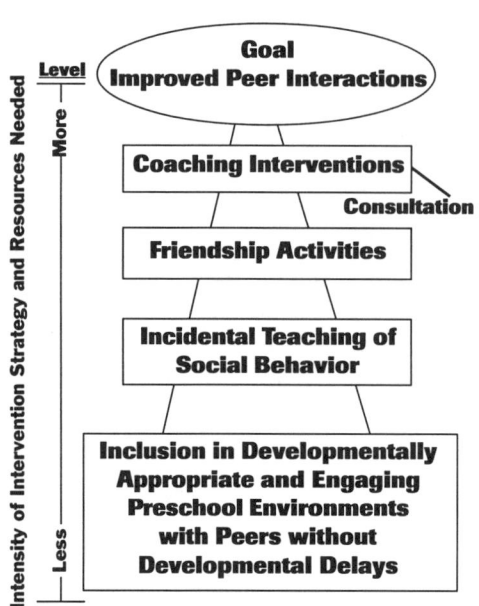

Figure 1. Strategies for Supporting and Promoting Preschool Children's Interactions

Our decision-making process has been intended to be sequential in nature in that we have encouraged early childhood educators to employ the least intrusive and most normalized type of intervention (i.e., intervention requiring fewer changes in classroom routines and activities with the least amount of additional resources) and, if necessary, to then proceed to a slightly more intensive intervention that might involve relatively simple program modifications (cf. Noonan & McCormick, 1993; Wolery, Strain, & Bailey, 1992). For example, we have suggested that an initial peer interaction strategy should be inclusion of young children with peer interaction difficulties in developmentally appropriate and engaging preschool programs (cf. Odom & Brown, 1993). Once children with developmental delays have become familiar with their peers, if they continue to have peer interaction problems, we have recommended that teachers implement incidental teaching of social behavior, a naturalistic teaching strategy, to promote young children's positive peer interactions (e.g., Brown, McEvoy, & Bishop, 1991).[5] Given the Promoting and Supporting Preschool Children's Peer Interactions hierarchy, if incidental teaching of social behavior is not sufficient to improve children's peer interactions, we have suggested that friendship activities (e.g., Brown, Ragland, & Bishop, 1989b), which are teacher-planned activities, should be used to augment both an inclusive placement and incidental teaching of social behavior. If across time, inclusive placement, incidental teaching, and friendship activities are not sufficient to improve children's peer interactions, we have recommended that teachers employ coaching strategies, which are conducted in small group sessions and are more teacher directed than incidental teaching and friendship activities, as an intensive strategy to facilitate young children's positive peer interactions. Although developed independently, the Strategies for Promoting and Supporting Preschool Children's Peer Interactions hierarchy has been similar to and compatible with recommendations of other early childhood educators who have advocated the use of less directive procedures first when promoting children's social interactions (cf. Bricker & Cripe, 1992; Noonan & McCormick, 1993; Nourot & Van Hoorn, 1991).

We believe that important aspects of our decision-making process have been that interventions should be:

Thirteen Critical Peer-related Social Competencies for Preschool Children

1. <u>Sharing Materials and Toys</u>. Two or more children are exchanging materials, toys, or objects in a positive manner within proximity to one another. This behavior includes offering or giving an object to another child or mutually using an object with another child. For example, two children are building a house with Legos, two children are looking at a book.

2. <u>Initiating Positive Interactions</u>. A child initiates to a peer by either physically touching, making eye contact, or verbally talking to the peer. For example, one child says "hi" to another child or a child puts her arm around another child.

3. <u>Assisting peers</u>. A positive physical behavior where one child physically helps another child with a particular activity or skill. For example, one child helps another child climb up on a piece of play equipment or one child physically assist a child in carrying a heavy piece of play material (e.g., a block).

4. <u>Positively Responding to Initiations</u>. One child responds either verbally or physically to another child's initiation. For example, when one child asks another "would you like to play in the sand table?" The child responds by walking over and beginning to play in the sand table or saying "yes."

5. <u>Communicating Needs and Wants Appropriately</u>. A child asks the teacher or peer for help, assistance, etc. by either physically bringing them to the situation needing help or verbally requesting help. For example, a toy is out of reach and the target child pulls the teacher over to the toy and points or verbally asks for the toy.

6. <u>Ongoing Interactions with Peers</u>. A sequence of positive initiations and responses between two or more peers. For example, one child says "Let's play spaceship" to another child. The peer says "OK, I'll be the pilot." Both peers run over to the jungle gym and pretend to fly/ride on the "spaceship."

7. <u>Expressing Anger in an Appropriate Manner</u>. Child either demonstrates dislike for a particular situation by saying "no" verbally or physically shaking his head. Another appropriate manner for demonstrating is to turn away from the setting without being aggressive.

8. <u>Taking Turns</u>. When two or more peers are sharing an object or a toy or participating in a game, the children allow each child to perform the specific action associated with the activity by waiting appropriately.

9. <u>Playing Cooperatively</u>. When two or more peers are playing together during a specific activity for a period of time, they may be sharing toys and materials or assisting each other, but each peer is acting in a positive manner during ongoing interaction.

10. <u>Demonstrating and Receiving Affection</u>. Any positive physical behavior where one child exhibits affectionate behavior toward another by patting, hugging, etc.

11. <u>Organizing Play Activities</u>. A positive verbal behavior where a child assigns a role for herself or another child or maintains an ongoing activity. This includes stating a rule or procedure for a game and a command for another child to participate in an organized activity.

12. <u>Refusing Initiations Appropriately</u>. When a child refuses another child's initiation by saying "no" or shaking his head "no" or turning away without being aggressive.

13. <u>Rough and Tumble Play</u>. Physical behavior where one child exhibits topographically "aggressive behavior" toward another child but the play behavior is accompanied by a positive affect from both participants. Can include behaviors such as "wrestling," "mock fighting," and "chasing."

Table 2[7].

- effective (i.e., clearly improve children's peer interactions);
- efficient (i.e., make good use of children's and teachers' time);
- functional (i.e., promote generalization and maintenance of important social competencies); and
- normalized (i.e., the most natural techniques possible) (cf. Carta, Schwartz, Atwater, & McConnell, 1991; Noonan & McCormick, 1993; Wolery et al., 1992).

In addition, at each level of the decision-making hierarchy (i.e., inclusive placement, incidental teaching, friendship activities, coaching interventions), we have recommended that the teachers carefully evaluate whether children's peer interactions have improved (e.g., increases in frequency of peer interactions, more positive peer interactions, more elaborate and sophisticated peer interactions). If peer interactions have not improved markedly, then the next more intensive level of intervention will be needed to enhance children's social interactions. Similar to initial identification, we have recommended that teachers employ relatively simple observational procedures to determine whether children's peer interactions have improved during routine preschool activities in common settings. If the current types of intervention have not promoted young children's peer interactions, then the next level of intervention should be implemented (e.g., implement friendship activities in addition to inclusive placement and incidental teaching). Periodic, direct observations of children in routine activities across the year will allow teachers to ascertain if their use of the current intervention strategies has promoted and supported young children's peer interactions. Moreover, periodic observations will inform teachers about whether children have maintained and elaborated their newly acquired peer-related social competencies.

We strongly recommend, however, that direct observation be employed as a primary method to determine whether children's peer interactions have improved (see Hill, 1992; Odom & Munson, 1996; Schwartz & Olswang, 1996; Wolery, 1996 for further information concerning observational methods). In the following section, we will discuss each level of our Strategies for Promoting and Supporting Preschool Children's Peer Interactions decision-making hierarchy in greater detail.

Developmentally Appropriate and Engaging Environments

For all most a decade, early childhood educators have developed and published guidelines for providing high-quality early childhood services (e.g., Bredekamp, 1987; Bredekamp & Rosegrant, 1992a; NAEYC & NAECS/SDE, 1991). These guidelines have provided a flexible framework that focuses on educators establishing developmentally appropriate and responsive early childhood environments. Unfortunately, some early childhood teachers have viewed Developmentally Appropriate Practice (DAP) as a manual or a "cook book" curriculum as opposed to thoughtful general guidelines of what constitutes recommended practices for young children (cf. Bredekamp & Rosegrant, 1992b; Richarz, 1993).

Many early childhood and early childhood special educators have asserted that the principles of DAP have served as a practical framework for programs that serve children with and without developmental delays (e.g., Brown, 1995; Cavallaro, Haney, & Cabello, 1993; Conroy et al., 1996; Diamond, Hestenes, & O'Conner, 1994; Guralnick, 1993; Wolery et al., 1992). Indeed, many early childhood special educators have readily recognized the importance of DAP as a curricular foundation for providing services to young children with developmental delays and their families (e.g., Atwater, Carta, Schwartz, & McConnell, 1994; DEC Task Force on Recommended Practices, 1993; McLean & Odom, 1996; Wolery et al., 1992; Wolery & Wilbers, 1994). In particular, with the two cardinal principles of DAP, *age appropriateness and individual appropriateness* (emphasis added), early childhood special educators have noted that the DAP guidelines are adaptable enough to permit the implementation of well-planned individual assessments (e.g., direct observation of social behavior, behavioral rating scales, developmental assessments) that link directly with classroom curricula and individualized interventions (e.g., Guralnick, 1993). We believe, however, that it has been critical (and will continue to be) for educators to understand that *individualized intervention* does not necessarily mean that only a single child will be the focus of or involved in intervention; nor that a child will be taught in a one-to-one teaching format. Rather, individualized intervention has presumed that children were assessed individually (at least with respect to analyzing their assessment information) and that one or more children's individual needs require additional intervention strategies to promote their further development. In preschool classrooms with young children with developmental delays, one, or two, or all the children might be participants in and benefit from individualized interventions that are implemented to meet the needs of one or more peers.

With respect to peer-related social competence, our understanding of DAP has indicated that developmentally appropriate preschool environments should be supportive of young children's social interactions with peers (cf. Bredekamp, 1987; Bredekamp & Rosegrant, 1992b). For example, developmentally appropriate programs have been arranged with activity or learning centers (e.g., kitchen/housekeeping, dramatic/pretend play, small manipulatives, blocks, literacy/books) that support most young children's active engagement with materials and peers (cf. Conroy et al., 1996; Isbell, 1995). We, along with others, have argued that the presence of appropriate classroom materials (e.g., Beckman & Kohl, 1984; Lieber & Beckman, 1991), well-planned learning centers (e.g., Isbell, 1995; Petrakos & Howe, 1996), and responsive teachers (e.g., Bredekamp & Rosegrant, 1992b) as recommended by the DAP guidelines are necessary conditions for enhancing young children's development (cf. Brown, 1995; Conroy et al., 1996). Moreover, these setting characteristics can promote and support young children's peer interactions and peer-related social competence (see Sainato & Carta, 1992 for a review of classroom influences).

Indeed, a long-standing reason for preschool inclusion has been to provide young children with developmental delays with socially supportive and developmentally engaging preschool environments (cf. Bricker, 1978; 1993). For young children with developmental delays, the presence of young children *without* developmental difficulties has been critical to providing to both peer models of competent behavior and socially responsive playmates (e.g., Guralnick, Connor, Hammond, Gottman, & Kinnish, 1995; Odom & Brown, 1993). Within socially active and responsive preschool settings, children have observed, practiced, and acquired important social behavior that was necessary for further development of their peer-related social competence (cf. Odom & Brown, 1993). Moreover, the activities conducted in many preschool programs and the existing social dynamics (as well as potential social dynamics) found in most early childhood settings, provide an ideal context for promoting and supporting young children's peer interactions, particularly for young children who have difficulties in their social development (cf. Mize, 1995, Odom & Brown, 1993). As Ladd and Coleman (1993) suggested, two important pathways for improved peer-related social competence are access (i.e., opportunities to interact with competent peers) and a rich history of positive peer interactions (i.e., frequent child-child interactions with multiple peers across time). Developmentally appropriate preschool environments that are engaging socially and that support young children's peer interactions can provide these two critical routes for preschool children's social development (cf. Brown, 1995). Hence, an initial strategy for early childhood educators who serve young children with and without developmental delays should be to implement and maintain the widely recognized DAP guidelines. If teachers' direct observations of their children have indicated that one or more children have peer interaction difficulties, as made explicit by our decision-making hierarchy, we have recommended the use of two naturalistic intervention strategies, which will be discussed in the next two subsections, to improve preschoolers' social interactions with peers.

Incidental Teaching of Social Behavior.

One effective naturalistic intervention strategy for improving young children's language and social behavior has been incidental teaching. For over two decades, incidental teaching has been used to promote young children's language development (see Hart, 1985; Kaiser, Yoder, & Keetz, 1992 for reviews). In recent years, incidental teaching of social behavior has been recommended as a strategy to improve young children's social interactions (e.g., Brown et al., 1991; Brown & Odom, 1995; McGee, Almeida, Sulzer-Azaroff, & Feldman, 1992). Incidental teaching has been differentiated from teacher-directed instruction because it has been employed during "...unstructured activities for brief periods of time and typically when children have shown an interest in or have been involved with materials, activities, or others" (Brown & Odom, 1995, p. 40).

Routine preschool activities such as free choice in learning centers, outdoor play, snack, transitions between activities, and arriving and leaving preschool have provided excellent circumstances in which incidental teaching of social behavior can be conducted. During incidental teaching episodes, teachers have promoted and supported children's peer interactions by providing adult models of suitable social behavior and encouraging peers to model appropriate social behavior. In addition, teachers have "fine tuned" (i.e., shaped) children's peer interactions by encouraging children to expand and elaborate their social behavior (e.g., in addition to physically comforting a peer who is upset—verbally expressing sympathy).

Episodes of incidental teaching of social behavior represent additional, albeit brief, teaching and learning opportunities for children to learn new peer-related social behaviors or practice and possibly elaborate previously acquired social responses during common preschool activities (cf. Brown et al., 1991). For example, Sam, a four-year-old child with mental retardation and accompanying peer interaction difficulties, sometimes interacts with his peer during structured large group activities such as "show and tell activities." Sam's teachers note through their classroom observations that during free choice activities in learning centers and in other less structured situations, Sam rarely initiates to his peers. During a free choice activity in the block center, one of Sam's teachers observes him watching LaShante building houses with large wooden blocks. Sam's teacher immediately encourages him to remember how to ask others to share toys and materials. Sam moves closer to LaShante and ask, "Me play?" LaShante says, "Sure, let's build a fire station!" while handing Sam some blocks. Sam and LaShante construct a pretend fire house while talking and giggling.

Across several months, during common classroom activities, whenever Sam has shown interest in materials, activities, or peers, his teachers continue to adeptly encourage his peer interactions. They note in their observations that Sam is beginning to ask peers to play and share without adult encouragement. In addition, without teacher prompting, peers are asking Sam to play with them during free choice activities. In spite of Sam's developmental delays, he has become socially engaged with his classmates and is now socially included in many classroom activities. Helpful hints for using incidental teaching of social behavior are delineated in Table 3 and additional examples of incidental teaching of social behavior are presented in Table 4.

Following inclusion of children within developmentally appropriate and engaging preschool environments, in addition to serving as a second level of intervention to improve children's peer interactions, incidental teaching of social behavior can serve another important purpose. Incidental teaching can be used to assess whether children need more intensive intervention strategies to promote their peer interactions (i.e., brief assessment or probe of children's peer-related social competence) (cf. Brown & Odom, 1995). For example, with children who have peer interaction difficulties that are verified by direct observation, if they fail to interact with peers during incidental teaching episodes with teacher support (i.e., well-timed and competent encouragement to interact with peers), then it is unlikely that they will socialize with peers in less structured preschool activities.[6] A lack of social responsiveness during incidental teaching may indicate that more frequent incidental teaching episodes may be needed or that relatively more intensive intervention strategies may be required (e.g., friendship activities, coaching).

McGee et al. (1992) and Nordquist, Twardosz, and McEvoy (1985) demonstrated that incidental teaching of social behavior has promoted peer interactions with a range of young children with and without developmental delays in an integrated preschool programs. For example, McGee and her colleagues (1992, 1995) employed frequent incidental teaching of social behavior as both an individual and classroom intervention to improve peer interactions among preschoolers with sig-

Helpful Hints for Implementing Incidental Teaching of Social Behavior

1. Identify children who will benefit from additional opportunities to interact with peers during preschool activities. Initially, teachers should identify children who might benefit from incidental teaching of social behavior by nomination. Specifically, teachers should rank order the children in their programs by the frequency of their positive peer interactions (i.e., first child with highest rate of positive peer interaction, second child with the next highest rate of positive peer interaction, third child with the next highest rate of peer interactions and so on. This should allow teachers to select those children who are the least verbal and seldom interct with peers. After ranking children, teachers should observe children during preschool activities that produce the most frequent child-child interaction episodes (e.g., freeplay outside, center time). The purpose of the observations is to confirm whether the selected children need frequent incidental teaching of social behavior to improve their peer interactions.

2. Identify common preschool activities and circumstances (e.g., play, transitions, arrival, center time) that will allow teachers to employ incidental teaching of social behavior with children.

3. Plan a variety of methods to actively encourage peer interactions. For example, some children may need physical assistance (e.g., walking hand-in-hand with a child to an activity center to play with another child), direct verbal encouragement (e.g., "Howard, ask Sam to share trucks with you!"), and indirect reminders (e.g., "Bill, remember how to ask Shelly to play?").

4. Implement incidental teaching episodes when you have enough time to observe and respond to children and their peers during common preschool activities and circumstances. Some activities and time periods are less conducive for promoting peer interaction. Typically, incidental teaching of social behavior should be performed during less structured circumstances and teaching episodes should be brief in duration.

5. Be sensitive and "follow the child's lead" by letting the child identify situations in which incidental teaching might be used. Children often indicate their interests in activities, materials, and peers by being in proximity and observing activities, materials, and peers. For example, if a child frequently stands near another child or a toy she may be very interested in the peer or toy.

6. Provide teacher support by systematically encouraging children who are selected for incidental teaching of social behavior to socially interact with peers who are more socially sophisticated. After teacher encouragement, if children socially interact with one another, teachers should explicity acknowledge those peer interactions with praise (e.g., "You guys made a wonderful fire station!").

7. Make peer interactions as pleasant, fun, and positive as possible. Be prepared to redirect children if their peer interaction becomes disruptive. Some children may require more teacher assistance and supervision while they play cooperatively. Across time, teachers should astutely withdraw from the peer interactions as children have more frequent positive interactions.

Table 3.

nificant social and language disorders (i.e., autism) in an integrated preschool program. Nevertheless, incidental teaching might not be sufficient to enhance some children's social behavior, and two additional intervention strategies, which are more intensive, may be needed to promote young children's peer interactions. Friendship activities and coaching strategies will be discussed in subsequent subsections.

Friendship Activities

Another naturalistic intervention strategy that has improved young children's social behavior has been friendship activities. Friendship activities have also been known as "group affection activities" (McEvoy et al., 1988; Twardosz, Nordquist, Simon, & Botkin, 1983) and "group socialization procedures" (Brown, Ragland, & Fox, 1988). Friendship activities have been differentiated from other social competence interventions because teachers modify young children's preschool environments to support peer interactions by using antecedent and consequent events during routine songs, games, and activities.

Antecedents and consequences used by teachers during friendship activities include:
- encouragement of children's peer interactions
- adult and peer modeling of prosocial behavior with opportunities for children to observe peer interactions
- behavioral rehearsal and practice of important social responses
- acknowledgment of and praise for children's peer interactions.

When teachers have employed friendship activities, they adapted routine preschool activities so that they systematically promote and support children's social behavior with peers during songs, games, or other group activities. Specifically, teachers have encouraged children's affectionate responding, complimenting, smiling, giving one another five or a thumbs up, dancing with one another, and sharing. During friendship activities, children's prosocial responding has been explicitly incorporated into common preschool activities within the daily classroom curriculum. Hence, friendship activities have been used as an intervention for all children in a preschool program and not just preschoolers with peer interaction problems. Friendship activities have been similar to activity-based programming in that they are teacher planned, embed teaching and learning episodes within common preschool activities, and use natural antecedents and consequences to promote further peer interaction among children [see chapter by Cripe & Lee, 1997, in this book for review].

In addition to the practical aspect of being easily implemented by teachers within common activities, several program components of friendship activities may have promoted generalization and maintenance of young children's social behavior (Brown et al., 1988; see Brown & Odom, 1994 for discussion of generalization strategies and tactics).

As a naturalistic peer interaction intervention strategy, friendship activities have three important advantages. First, when teachers conduct friendship activities, they transform their preschool classrooms to enhance young children's peer interactions and the formation of friendships. Specifically, teachers systematically encourage children to participate in

Activity	Incidental Teaching Direction by the Teacher	Child Interactive Response	Anticipated Response from Peer(s)
PLAY Billy is playing with blocks and Susie (target child) is standing and watching.	'Susie, why don't you play with Billy?' 'Billy, share the blocks with Susie.'	Susie sits down next to Billy Susie and says, 'Me play too.'	Susie begins to build a block fort with Billy.
LUNCH David (target child) needs help opening a milk carton.	'David, ask Dana to help you open your milk carton.'	'Dana, help me please.'	Dana helps David open his milk and David says 'Thanks, Dana.'
BATHROOM Teacher needs Brad (target child) to come and use the bathroom and wash his hands.	'Sam, go over to Brad and tell him it's time to use the bathroom. Bring him over here.'	Sam says, 'Brad, it's time to use the bathroom, let's go over there.'	Sam walks with Brad toward the bathroom and says, 'You can go first, Brad.' Brad signs, 'Okay.'
TRANSITION Bill (target child) need his chair moved from table activities to large group.	'Susie, will you be a good friend and help Bill move his chair to large group?'	Susie says, 'Bill, I'll help you. Where do you want to sit today?'	Bill walks to large group with his walker and points next to Susie's chair while Susie moves his chair next to hers.
ARRIVAL Todd (target child) has trouble with the buttons on his coat when he comes to school.	'David, remember Todd has trouble unbuttoning his coat. Will you go and help him?'	David approaches Todd and says, 'Todd, you want me to unbutton your coat? Watch *me*.'	Todd nods his head yes and approaches David. Todd watches David unbutton his buttons and hangs his coat up and then hugs David.
CLASSTIME Howard is walking from large group to the snack table and falls down.	'Oh, Mary (target child), look, Howard fell down. Let's help him up and give him a hug.'	Mary and the teacher walk over and help Howard stand up. Mary hugs Howard.	Howard hugs Mary and says, 'Let's go eat snack.'
FINE MOTOR ACTIVITY Paul (target child), who is mute but can work complex connecting puzzles, is working a 20-piece puzzle.	'Look, Paul, Al needs help with his puzzle. Show him how to work it.'	Paul shows Al where a piece of the puzzle goes and smiles.	Paul and Al take turns putting pieces of the puzzle in. After completing the puzzle Al says, 'We did it.'

Table 4. Examples of Possible Incidental Teaching of Social Behavior

prosocial activities within the context of common classroom activities. Second, teachers promote children's rehearsal of a number of important social behaviors during a variety of activities with multiple peers in typical preschool settings. The teaching tactic of "training loosely" without decontextualizing peer interactions may be critical for enhancing generalization and maintenance of children's social behavior (cf. Brown & Odom, 1994). Finally, friendship activities include regular discussion of the importance of peer interactions and friendships, and those discussions establish and help maintain a supportive atmosphere for peer interactions and the formation of children's social relationships. Importantly, discussions of the importance of friendships and teacher encouragement of peer interactions can be embedded within most preschool games, songs, and activities.

Similar to incidental teaching of social behavior, friendship activities represent additional teaching and learning opportunities for children to learn new peer-related social responses or practice and possibly elaborate previously acquired social behaviors during common preschool activities (cf. Brown et al., 1989a). Because friendship activities are teacher planned and are conducted with groups of children, they provide more teaching and learning opportunities for children to participate in peer interactions and to observe other children's involvement in peer interactions than incidental teaching. Hence, friendship activities constitute a more intensive intervention strategy than incidental teaching. We encourage the continuation of incidental teaching after friendship activities are initiated. Because friendship activities are teacher planned and include more adult support for children's social interactions, incidental teaching of social behavior episodes will continue to provide an important "bridge" for transferring children's newly acquired social behaviors to less structured preschool activities and situations. That is, incidental teaching episodes may be used to promote generalization and maintenance of children's peer-related social competence to less structured and adult-directed circumstances.

Similar to most preschool activities, teachers enthusiasm has been critical to successful implementation of friendship activities. In previous field tests, teachers reported feeling slightly awkward when initially encouraging children to interact with peers more extensively during songs, games, and other preschool activities (Brown et al., 1989a). This initial teacher reaction was probably not surprising considering we asked teachers to alter slightly their methods of conducting preschool activities. Across relatively short periods of time, however, those same teachers noted that as they participated in friendship activities with the children they became more comfortable and enjoyed the activities along with their preschool students.

As an example of a friendship activity, with minor modifications, the children's game "Duck, Duck, Goose," can be become an excellent activity to promote peer interactions and friendships by providing children with multiple opportunities to participate in or observe others interacting positively with peers. Traditionally, "Duck, Duck, Goose" is played in preschools and children sit or stand in a circle. One child walks around the circle gently touching each participant and saying "Duck!" At some point in time, the child, who is walking around saying "Duck!," surprises the other children and says "Goose!" The peer who is gently touched when "Goose" was said then chases the touching child around the circle trying to catch her before they return to the chasing child's place in the circle. Children have enjoyed this simple game for decades and have learned important competencies such as listening closely, waiting one's turn, following basic rules of games, self-control when one is not picked as the "Goose" or does not win (i.e., catch the child), observing others, and so on.

With appropriate support from preschool teachers, "Duck, Duck, Goose" can become a friendship activity. Teachers should prepare children for the changes involved in the "Duck, Duck, Goose" friendship activities. Before each game, teachers should discuss the importance of positive peer interactions and friendships. In addition, teachers should describe how the children will be asked to play the game with the accompanying requests to interact positively with peers. Both teacher and peer models of the prosocial behaviors that

---

Helpful Hints for Implementing Friendship Activities

1. **Identify children who will benefit from additional opportunities to interact with peers during preschool activities.** Similar to identifying children for incidental teaching episodes, teachers should identify children who might benefit from friendship activities by nomination and follow-up observations to verify the need for further peer interaction intervention.

2. **Identify common preschool activities, songs, and games that will allow you to embed teacher encouragement to interact with peers and teacher-explicit acknowledgment of those interactions into selected preschool activities.** Because friendship activities are meant to augment preschool curricula, they should be performed during activities that typically occur during the daily schedule.

3. **Before implementation of friendship activities, teachers should determine:** (a) who are the participating children (both target children and socially sophisticated peers); (b) when will the friendship activities be performed; (c) which preschool activities will be employed as the context for facilitating children's peer interactions; and (d) what materials (if any) will be needed to conduct friendship activities.

4. **Before initial implementation of friendship activities, teachers should prepare participating children by discussing how the group activities will change** (i.e., explicit encouragement to socially interact with peers, teacher acknowledgment of peer interactions) and the purpose of the changes (i.e., "to become better friends").

5. **Before the start of every friendship activity, teachers should remind children of the purpose of friendship activities and discuss the importance of positive social interactions and making friends.**

6. **Similar to incidental teaching of social behavior, plan a variety of methods to actively encourage peer interactions** (e.g., physical assistance if needed, verbal prompts to interact).

7. **Provide on-going teacher support by systematically encouraging target children who are to socially interact with peers who are more socially sophisticated.** During friendship activities, if children socially interact with one another, you should explicitly acknowledge those peer interactions with praise.

8. **Make peer interactions as pleasant, fun, and positive as possible.** Be prepared to calm children down or to redirect them if their peer interactions become disruptive.

Table 5.

teachers are encouraging (e.g., compliments, sharing, positive comments) are helpful in providing children with a better understanding of the changes in the game. Although all children are participants in the game, adept teachers will unobtrusively focus their encouragements and acknowledgments on children who they know have peer interaction difficulties. Basically, a primary purpose of friendship activities is to provide additional teaching and learning opportunities with appropriate teacher support to children with peer interaction problems. Within the context of the friendship activities, socially sophisticated peers can provide important assistance in promoting withdrawn children's peer interactions. Moreover, with discussions of friendship and many opportunities to interact, the preschool atmosphere has become favorable for children's peer interactions and the formation of friendships.

Friendship activities have been an effective method for improving young children's peer interaction. For example, Twardosz et al. (1983) demonstrated that friendship activities facilitated the peer interactions of preschool children who were socially withdrawn. Brown et al. (1988) and McEvoy et al. (1988) replicated Twardosz and colleagues' initial findings with children with significant developmental delays (e.g., autism, mental retardation, emotional disturbance). Helpful hints for using friendship activities are delineated in Table 5.

Both incidental teaching of social behavior and friendship activities have been naturalistic peer interaction interventions that have been easily integrated into preschool programs for children with and without developmental delays. Importantly, these two naturalistic strategies have been socially beneficial to many children with wide ranges of developmental abilities (i.e., from normal development to children with significant developmental delays). Teachers who employed incidental teaching and friendship activities adapted young children's preschool environments to become more socially supportive of children's peer interactions and peer relations by systematically encouraging and acknowledging children's social interactions. Although incidental teaching of social behavior and friendship activities have not been as structured as other social interaction interventions, along with inclusion of young children with peer interaction difficulties in developmentally appropriate and engaging preschool environments, they represent two reasonable approaches for early childhood teachers who are interested in improving young children's peer interactions prior to implementing more intensive coaching interventions. Moreover, as we have suggested with our support hierarchy, these naturalistic intervention strategies may be sufficient support to enhance many preschool children's peer interactions (cf. Brown et al., 1988; Brown et al., 1991). Nevertheless, for some young children with peer interaction difficulties, incidental teaching of social behavior and friendship activities might not be sufficient to promote their social behavior, and coaching intervention strategies (e.g., Mize, 1995; Odom & McConnell, 1993), which are more structured and intensive, may be needed to promote preschoolers' peer interactions. Two small group coaching strategies will be discussed in the next subsection.

Coaching Interventions

During the last decade, social competence researchers have developed and refined social competence intervention programs for preschool children (see Odom & Brown, 1993; McEvoy, Odom, & McConnell, 1992 for recent reviews). Two contemporary examples of small group social competence interventions have been a cognitive-social learning intervention model (Mize, 1995) and *Play Time/Social Time* (Odom & McConnell, 1993). These two social competence curricula have been designed to remediate young children's peer-related social competence difficulties by improving preschoolers. These include knowledge of critical social competencies and performance of specific behavioral strategies related to peer interactions.

Relative to incidental teaching of social behavior and friendship activities, a cognitive-social learning intervention model and *Play Time/Social Time* have been more intensive and have required more teacher planning, direction, and monitoring of specific social behaviors. Other formal social competence programs have been available for preschool children (see Table 6).

A cognitive-social learning intervention model. Mize (1995) described a systematic approach, which she calls a cognitive-social learning model, for early childhood educators who want to improve young children's peer interactions. The young children involved in her field test of a cognitive-social learning intervention model included preschool children with low social status as indicated by sociometric assessment and direct observation of play activities and peers who were typically developing. With respect to content of the curriculum, Mize recommended focusing on four social behaviors that are frequently used by preschool children to initiate, maintain, and elaborate their peer interactions and social play. Specifically, she has targeted prosocial leading, asking questions, commenting on play, and offering peer support as critical social competencies for intervention. She has not limited the content of intervention to those four social behaviors, however. Indeed, she noted that teachers "...should encourage preschool-age children to use specific verbal behaviors described in this section, as well as those identified through observation during peer interaction." (Mize, 1995, p. 241).

The cognitive-social learning intervention model described by Mize (1995) has three fundamental components:

- social knowledge
- performance proficiency
- monitoring and self-evaluation.

Obviously, children who lack appropriate social knowledge have been at high risk for peer rejection and failure to form friendships. Typically, well-liked children have employed their social knowledge effectively with peers. Some children, particularly rejected children, however, have frequently used ineffective or inappropriate behavioral strategies with their peers in social situations. For example, when introduced to new play situations with unfamiliar peers, many preschool children have "hovered" in proximity and watched other young children while they play. Occasionally, they have smiled or commented on what the other children are doing (e.g., "What a cool car!"). On the other hand, some children with immature social knowledge and social behavior have summarily "snatched" toys and have gone and played with the toys alone (cf. Kopp et al., 1992). Obviously, children who have frequently taken peers' toys have been at risk for peer rejection.

Additional Social Competence Resources

Articles, Chapters, and Books
Goldstein, H., & Cisar, C. L. (1992). Promoting interaction during sociodramatic play: Teaching scripts to typical preschoolers and classmates with disabilities. Journal of Applied Behavior Analysis, 25, 265-280.

Kohler, F. W., McCullough, K. M., & Buchan, K. A. (1995). Using peer coaching to enhance preschool teachers' development and refinement of classroom activities. Early Education and Development, 6, 215-239.

McEvoy, M. A., & McConnell, S. R. (1995). Understanding the emotional and behavioral development of young children: 3-6 years. In T. Zirpoli (Ed.), Understanding and affecting the behavior of young children (pp. 60-81). Columbus, OH: Merrill.

McEvoy, M. A., & Odom, S. L. (1996). Strategies for promoting social interaction and emotional development of infants and young children with disabilities and their families. In S. L. Odom & M. E. McLean (Eds.), Early intervention/early childhood special education: Recommended practices (pp. 223-244). Austin, TX: PRO-ED.

Odom, S. L., McConnell, S. R., & McEvoy, M. A. (1992). Social competence of young children with disabilities: Issues and strategies for intervention. Baltimore: Paul H. Brookes.

Potential Preschool Social Competence Curricula
Brown, W. H., Ragland, E. U., & Bishop, N. (1989). A socialization curriculum for preschool programs that integrate children with handicaps. Nashville, TN: John F. Kennedy Center for Research on Human Development, Peabody College of Vanderbilt University.

Cartledge, G., & Kleefeld, J. (1991). Taking part: Introducing social skills to children. Circle Pines, MN: American Guidance Service.

English, K., Goldstein, H., Kaczmarek, L., & Shafer, K. (1996). "Buddy Skills" for preschoolers. Teaching Exceptional Children, 28, 62-66.

Linder, T. W. (1993). Transdisciplinary play-based intervention: Guidelines for developing a meaningful curriculum for young children. Baltimore: Paul H. Brookes.

Mize, J. (1995). Coaching preschool children in social skills: A cognitive-social learning curriculum. In G. Cartledge & J. F. Milburn (Eds.), Teaching social skills to children and youth: Innovative approaches (pp. 237-261). Boston: Allyn and Bacon.

Odom, S. L., & McConnell, S. R. (1993). Play Time/Social Time: Organizing your classroom to build interaction skills. Tucson, AZ: Communication Skills Builders.

Sheridan, M. K., Foley, G. M., & Radlinkski, S. H. (1995). Using the supportive play model: Individualized intervention in early childhood practice. New York: Teachers College Press.

Table 6

As Mize (1995) noted, many of young children's social interaction strategies "...are more script-based and automatic than reflective or thoughtful." (p. 244). That is, within common social situations, preschool children have tended to employ social strategies they have used before or have seen (cf. Mize & Ladd, 1990). Given young children's propensity for "script-based social strategies," Mize has argued for directly teaching children new behavioral strategies to replace maladaptive peer interactions with more effective ones. Moreover, because children's social scripts have been learned through frequent participation in or observation of effective social interaction sequences (cf. Nelson, 1981; Goldstein & Cisar, 1992), Mize recommended that teachers model and rehearse effective social scripts within small group, social skills intervention sessions (i.e., coaching sessions) (cf. Mize & Ladd, 1990; Mize, 1995). These relatively intensive training formats have included a coach (i.e., teacher), children with peer interaction difficulties, socially sophisticated peers, and puppets and other play materials. Within high interest sociodramatic play activities, children have been taught and encouraged to practice social interaction scripts (i.e., new social knowledge) that involve interacting positively with peers.

The second fundamental component of a cognitive-social learning intervention model has been performance proficiency. Mize cautioned that knowledge alone is not sufficient to promote positive peer interactions. She noted, "...failure to translate knowledge into action may result from ineptness, anxiety, or lack of practice." (Mize, 1995, p. 244). For example, a child may be able to describe an appropriate social interaction strategy with an adult but fail to use that strategy in appropriate classroom circumstances and contexts. Because initial coaching sessions have been conducted within small group formats, Mize advised teachers to plan for and support children's transfer of newly acquired social interaction scripts to routine preschool contexts and activities (i.e., plan for and promote generalization and maintenance). To assist children in generalizing newly acquired social knowledge, Mize recommended that teachers employ multiple peers during coaching sessions and that they systematically encourage children's performance of newly acquired social interaction scripts within routine classroom activities in natural contexts. In addition, Mize noted that teachers should monitor children's behavioral performance closely so that they can be sensitive and responsive to children's needs for adult support in common preschool activities.

The final component of a cognitive-social learning intervention model has been monitoring and self-evaluation. Effective and appropriate social behavior has required children to attend to and read social cues and social contexts. With respect to interpersonal cues and important contextual information, preschool children have only begun to self-monitor and self-evaluate, and they often require adult assistance in interpreting their social circumstances (cf. Vygotsky, 1978). Indeed, many funny circumstances (e.g., preschoolers literal interpretation of adults' statements) and problematic situations (e.g., preschoolers misreading peers' social signals) have resulted from young children's emerging and relatively less mature social cognition. Hence, many young children have benefited from teachers explicit interpretations of common peer reactions to their behavior (e.g., "When you don't share, it upsets your friends!"). In addition, adept teachers have provided adaptive interpretations of peers' negative or rejecting social behavior (e.g., "I believe he wants to play alone now."). Teachers' timely interpretations and continued support and encouragement have been needed to prevent chronic rejection by peers and to facilitate some children's future attempts to interact with peers. Moreover, teachers assistance and sensitivity have been required to break cycles of social rejection before negative social reputations have been established. Specific self-evaluation strategies have been effective with preschool children with and without developmental delays in promoting young children's peer interactions (e.g., Sainato, Goldstein, & Strain, 1992).

Mize also recommended that while implementing a cognitive-social learning intervention model, that coaches be enthusiastic and sensitive to children's individual needs. Moreover, coaches should avoid stigmatizing children by noting their social competence problems. Rather, children have been informed that their coach needs to better understand how children can have more fun while playing with one another. Within small group coaching sessions, with children with social competence difficulties and socially sophisticated peers, effective coaches have modeled appropriate social scripts and have had peers model appropriate social scripts while allowing children to rehearse those scripts during high interest play activities. Moreover, adept coaches have:
- provided multiple opportunities to practice and observe social scripts
- encouraged performance of social scripts both within the coaching sessions and in natural classroom contexts
- assisted children in better understanding and interpreting peers social behavior and peers social reactions to them.

Because competent social behavior is dependent on effective social-cognitive abilities, teachers who use a cognitive-social learning intervention model have taught children new social concepts and have supported them while they practiced and generalized their new social knowledge. Moreover, coaches have assisted children in more accurately interpreting their peers' behavior in common social circumstances (i.e., self-monitoring and self-evaluating). A cognitive-social learning intervention model has been effective with 29 preschoolers who had relatively mild peer-related social competence problems (e.g., social withdrawal, low peer status). Specifically, from pre-test to posttest, young children who participated in a cognitive-social learning curriculum doubled the frequency of their use of targeted social scripts whereas children who did not participate in the curriculum decreased their use of targeted behavioral strategies (Mize & Ladd, 1988; 1990). In addition, after completion of a cognitive-social learning curriculum, participating children suggested friendlier and more positive social interaction strategies to hypothetical social dilemmas than non-participating comparison children. It should be noted, however, to our knowledge, that a cognitive-social learning intervention model has not been used with preschool children with developmental delays (e.g., mental retardation, autism, language disorders). Given that a cognitive-social learning intervention model has required relatively sophisticated language and cognitive abilities, other intervention models may be more appropriate for young children with identified developmental delays. *Play Time/Social Time* (Odom & McConnell, 1993) has been a social competence program that has been effective with a number of preschool children with and without developmental delays, and the curriculum will be described in the next section.

Play Time/Social Time. Odom and McConnell (1993) and their colleagues developed and evaluated a curriculum, which they entitled *Play Time/Social Time*, for early childhood educators who want to improve young children's peer interactions. The preschool participants in their field tests included children with and without developmental delays. Specifically, Odom and McConnell and their colleagues developed detailed procedures for:

➡ assessing and identifying participants for their curriculum;

➡ arranging preschool environments to facilitate peer interactions and peer interaction interventions;

➡ teaching specific peer interaction strategies to children targeted for intervention and their peers;

➡ employing teacher prompts and feedback to ensure that peer interaction strategies are implemented during play activities; and

➡ making adaptations for use in various preschool settings and circumstances.

Play Time/Social Time was developed for three-, four-, and five-year-old children who are enrolled in early childhood special education and early childhood programs (e.g., preschools, Head Start Centers, child care centers). The peer-related social competence procedures were used with children at risk for developmental problems and children with identified developmental delays (e.g., mental retardation, autism, language disorders). In addition, the curriculum was also designed to be used with peers who are developing normally or who have relatively high levels of social competence in integrated and inclusive early childhood programs.

With respect to content of the curriculum, Odom and McConnell (1993) recommended focusing on six social behaviors that have been identified previously by researchers as critical peer interaction skills (e.g., Tremblay et al., 1981). Specifically, they targeted sharing, being persistent, requesting to share, organizing play, agreeing, and helping. The curriculum was field tested with 21 preschool teachers and over 100 young children with and without developmental delays. During the development of *Play Time/Social Time*, Odom and McConnell refined a comprehensive social competence intervention approach, which included environmental arrangements and child-focused and peer-mediated interventions, to facilitate peer interactions and peer-related social competence. Odom, McConnell, and colleagues have included specific sections in the curriculum on:

➡ understanding the problems related to peer-related social competence;

➡ selecting of participants for social competence intervention;

➡ employing the well-sequenced social skills lessons in preschool programs;

➡ programming for generalization; and

➡ adapting components of the curriculum for preschool classrooms.

Similar to Mize (1995), Odom and McConnell (1993) recommended that teachers enthusiastically implement peer interaction activities within a small group format with both children with peer-related social competence problems and more sophisticated peers. Like a cognitive-social learning intervention model, teachers systematically encourage children to employ the targeted social behaviors (e.g., sharing, play organizing) during high interest activities common to most preschool programs. *Play Time/Social Time* has had several strengths as a peer-related social competence curriculum. First, the curriculum was developed with the direct participation of and input from many preschool teachers. Second, the curriculum was well-sequenced with many specific recommendations and activities that make it a relatively comprehensive social skills program for preschool children. A third strong point of the curriculum was the specification of procedures for planning for generalization and maintenance of young children's newly acquired social competence abilities. Although *Play Time/Social Time* was developed with very specific and elaborate procedures, Odom and McConnell have recommended that teachers be flexible in the implementation of the curriculum. A final strength has been the inclusion of specific suggestions for adapting curriculum components and procedures.

As indicated by collection of several social competence measures (e.g., direct observation, sociometric assessments, teacher rating scales), *Play Time/Social Time* was effective in improving peer interactions of many preschool children with a wide range of developmental abilities (e.g., typically developing, mental retardation, developmental delays). In general, children who participated in the peer-related social competence interventions improved their peer interactions. The recommended comprehensive intervention program (i.e., environmental arrangement, child-focused and peer-initiated interventions) was as effective as previous child-focused and peer-mediated interventions (cf. Odom & McConnell, 1993). In addition, follow-up assessments with participants the next school year indicated that children who participated in comprehensive social competence intervention were performing socially at levels found at the end of the intervention (i.e., the previous spring) in spite of a summer break and without continued intensive intervention in the children's new classrooms. Given these positive results, *Play Time/Social Time* has been validated as an effective curriculum for children with and without developmental delays, particularly young children who may not have sophisticated language and cognitive abilities of children who participated in a cognitive-social learning model.

Conclusions and Recommendations

Many early childhood educators view children's peer interactions and peer-related social competence as critical aspects of young children's overall development (cf. Wolery et al., 1992; Guralnick, 1994; McConnell, McEvoy, & Odom, 1992; Odom, McConnell, & Chandler, 1994). Nevertheless, the implementation of peer-related social competence interventions in many early childhood programs has been limited (cf. McConnell et al., 1992). We believe that teachers should be proactive about promoting and supporting young children's peer interactions and peer-related social competence in preschool programs. Moreover, the Strategies for Promoting and Supporting Preschool Children's Peer Interactions hierarchy, which includes a continuum of intervention strategies, will provide teachers with a practical decision-making process for encouraging young children's peer interactions in inclusive early childhood programs.

While employing the decision-making hierarchy with periodic direct observations of children's peer interactions, teachers can evaluate whether more intensive intervention strategies will be needed to improve preschool children's peer interactions. Moreover, as teachers promote and support more frequent and elaborate peer interactions, children's peer-related social competence should improve. Ultimately, with children's increased peer interactions and improved peer-related social competence, children should begin to form more enduring friendships. We view the development of positive peer relations as an important goal for early childhood educators (cf. Haring, 1992; Hartup, 1992; Ladd & Coleman, 1993). Although we, along with others (e.g., Brown & Odom, 1993; Mallory & New, 1994; Wolery et al., 1992), conclude that young children with developmental delays and accompanying peer interaction difficulties should receive their early childhood services in community programs that adhere to developmentally appropriate practices, we also believe strongly that personnel in inclusive early childhood programs should be prepared to adapt curricular practices and, when necessary, to use a continuum of teaching strategies to assure that all children's developmental needs are being addressed (cf. Atwater, Carta, Schwartz, & McConnell, 1994; Carta et al., 1991; Wolery et al., 1992). In addition to establishing and maintaining developmentally appropriate and engaging environments, early childhood educators employment of naturalistic teaching procedures (e.g., incidental teaching of social behavior, friendship activities) and, when necessary, small group coaching strategies, should provide teachers with an effective array of peer-related social competence interventions.

The decision-making hierarchy we have advocated will allow teachers to employ peer-related social competence interventions that are only as intrusive as necessary to promote and support children's peer interactions in preschool settings. Our pragmatic approach to determining the intensity of peer-related social competence interventions is similar to that of other educators who have recognized that a variety of intervention strategies, which range in intensity level from child-initiated (e.g., incidental teaching) to teacher-directed (e.g., small group coaching) interventions, may be needed for children with developmental delays (cf. Bredekamp & Rosegrant, 1992b; Harris & Graham, 1994), particularly for preschool children with developmental delays and accompanying peer interaction difficulties in inclusive programs (cf. Atwater et al., 1994; Carta et al., 1991; Mallory & New, 1994; Wolery et al., 1992; Wolery & Wilbers, 1994). We sincerely believe that the employment of the Strategies for Promoting and Supporting Preschool Children's Peer Interactions hierarchy with the accompanying peer interaction intervention strategies will provide early childhood educators with a range of appropriate options for encouraging and supporting young children's peer interactions and peer-related social competence. Moreover, we hope the Strategies for Promoting and Supporting Preschool Children's Peer Interactions hierarchy will assist early childhood educators in *socially integrating* young children with developmental delays in inclusive preschool programs (cf. Odom & McEvoy, 1988).

Preparation of this chapter was supported by a Research and Productive Scholarship Grant from the University of South Carolina.

References

Asher, S. R. (1990). Recent advances in the study of peer rejection. In S. R. Asher & Coie, J. D. (Eds.). *Peer rejection in childhood* (pp. 3-14). New York: Cambridge University Press.

Atwater, J. B., Carta, J. J., Schwartz, I. S., & McConnell, S. R. (1994). Blending developmentally appropriate practice and early childhood special education: Redefining best practice to meet the needs of all children. In B. L. Mallory & R. S. New (Eds.), *Diversity & developmentally appropriate practices: Challenges for early childhood education* (pp. 185-201). New York: Teachers College Press.

Beckman, P. J., & Kohl, F. L. (1984). The effects of social and isolate toys on the interactions and play of integrated and nonintegrated groups of preschoolers. *Education and Training of the Mentally Retarded, 19,* 169-174.

Bijou, S. W. (1993). *Behavior analysis of child development* (Second Edition). Reno, NV: Context Press.

Bredekamp, S. (1987). *Developmentally appropriate practice in early childhood programs serving young children from birth through age 8.* Washington, DC: National Association for the Education of Young Children.

Bredekamp, S., & Rosegrant, T. (Eds.). (1992a). *Reaching potentials: Appropriate curriculum and assessment for young children.* Washington, DC: National Association for the Education of Young Children.

Bredekamp, S., & Rosegrant, T. (1992b). Reaching potentials: Introduction. In S. Bredekamp & T. Rosegrant (Eds.), *Reaching potentials: Appropriate curriculum and assessment for young children* (pp. 2-8). Washington, DC: National Association for the Education of Young Children.

Bricker, D. D. (1978). A rationale for the integration of handicapped and nonhandicapped preschool children. In M. J. Guralnick (Ed.), *Early intervention and the integration of handicapped and nonhandicapped children* (pp. 3-26). Baltimore: University Park Press.

Bricker, D. D. (1993). Integration: Campaign for the new century. In C. A. Peck, S. L. Odom, & D. Bricker (Eds.), *Integrating young children with disabilities into community programs: Ecological perspectives on research and implementation* (pp. 271-276). Baltimore: Paul H. Brookes.

Bricker, D., & Cripe, J. (1992). *An activity-based approach to early intervention.* Baltimore: Paul H. Brookes.

Brown, W. H. (1995). Inclusive therapeutic preschool programs for young children. *Dimensions of Early Childhood, 23,* 22-40.

Brown, W. H., & Conroy, M. A. (1997). Inclusion of preschool children with developmental delays in early childhood programs. In W. H. Brown & M. A. Conroy (Eds.), *Inclusion of preschool children with developmental delays in early childhood programs* (pp.). Little Rock, AR: Southern Early Childhood Association.

Brown, W. H., McEvoy, M. A., & Bishop, J. N. (1991). Incidental teaching of social behavior: A naturalistic approach to promoting young children's peer interactions. *Teaching Exceptional Children, 24,* 35-58.

Brown, W. H., & Odom, S. L. (1994). Strategies and tactics for promoting generalization and maintenance of young children's social behavior. *Research in Developmental Disabilities, 15,* 99-118.

Brown, W. H., & Odom, S. L. (1995). Naturalistic peer interventions for promoting preschool children's social interactions. *Preventing School Failure, 39,* 38-43.

Brown, W. H., Odom, S. L., & Holcombe, A. (1996). Observational assessment of young children's social behavior with peers. *Early Childhood Research Quarterly, 11,* 19-40.

Brown, W. H., Ragland, E. U., & Bishop, N. (1989a). *A socialization curriculum for preschool programs that integrate children with handicaps.* Nashville, TN: John F. Kennedy Center for Research on Human Development, Peabody College of Vanderbilt University.

Brown, W. H., Ragland, E. U., & Bishop, J. N. (1989b). A naturalistic teaching strategy to promote young children's peer interactions. *Teaching Exceptional Children, 21,* 8-10.

Brown, W. H., Ragland, E. U., & Fox, J. J. (1988). Effects of group socialization procedures on the social interactions of preschool children. *Research in Developmental Disabilities, 9,* 359-376.

Cavallaro, C. C., Haney, M., & Cabello, B. (1993). Developmentally appropriate strategies for promoting full participation in early childhood settings. *Topics in Early Childhood Special Education, 13,* 293-307.

Campbell, S. B. (1990). *Behavior problems in preschool children: Clinical and developmental issues.* New York: Guilford.

Carta, J. J., Schwartz, I. S., Atwater, J. B., & McConnell, S. R. (1991). Developmentally appropriate practice: Appraising its usefulness for young children with disabilities. *Topics in Early Childhood Special Education, 11,* 1-20.

Conroy, M. A., & Fox, J. J. (1995). An observational analysis and validation of social and survival skills for preschool and school aged children with and without disabilities. In S. L. Odom (Chair), *Understanding social competence of young children with and without developmental disabilities.* Symposium conducted at the Proceedings of the 28th Gatlinburg Conference on Research and Theory in Mental Retardation and Developmental Disabilities, Gatlinburg, Tennessee.

Conroy, M. A., Langenbrunner, M. R., & Burleson, R. B. (1996). Suggestions for enhancing the social behaviors of preschoolers with disabilities: Using Developmentally Appropriate Practices. *Dimensions of Early Childhood, 24,* 9-15.

Cripe, J. J., & Lee, J. (1996). Activity-based intervention strategies for preschool children with developmental delays in early childhood programs. In W. H. Brown & M. A. Conroy (Eds.), *Inclusion of preschool children with developmental delays in early childhood programs* (pp.). Little Rock, AR: Southern Early Childhood Association.

DEC Task Force on Recommended Practices. (1993). *DEC recommended practices: Indicators of quality in programs for infants and young children with special needs and their families.* Reston, VA: Council for Exceptional Children.

Diamond, K. E., Hestenes, L. L., & O'Conner, C. E. (1994). Integrating young children with disabilities in preschool: Problems and promises. *Young Children, 49,* 68-73.

Flavel, J. H. (1977). *Cognitive development.* Englewood Cliffs, NJ: Prentice-Hall, Inc.

Goldstein, H., & Cisar, C. L. (1992). Promoting interaction during sociodramatic play: Teaching scripts to typical preschoolers and classmates with disabilities. *Journal of Applied Behavior Analysis, 25,* 265-280.

Greenwood, C. R., Walker, H. M., Todd, N. M., & Hops, H. (1979). Selecting a cost-effective screening device for the assessment of preschool social withdrawal. *Journal of Applied Behavior Analysis, 12,* 639-652.

Guralnick, M. J. (1992). A hierarchical model for understanding children's peer-related social competence. In S. L. Odom, S. R. McConnell, & M. A. McEvoy (Eds.), *Social competence of young children with disabilities: Issues and strategies for intervention* (pp. 37-64). Baltimore: Paul H. Brookes.

Guralnick, M. J. (1993). Developmentally appropriate practice in the assessment and intervention of children's peer relations. *Topics in Early Childhood Special Education, 13,* 344-371.

Guralnick, M. J. (1994). Social competence with peers: Outcome and process in early childhood special education. In P. L. Safford (Ed.), *Yearbook in Early Childhood Education: Early Childhood Special Education* (vol. 5) (pp. 45-71). New York: Teachers College Press.

Guralnick, M. J., Connor, R. T., Hammond, M., Gottman, J. M., & Kinnish, K. (1995). Immediate effects of mainstreamed settings on the social interactions and social integration of preschool children. *American Journal of*

Mental Retardation, 100, 359-377.

Haring, T. G. (1992). The context of social competence: Relations, relationships, and generalization. In S. L. Odom, S. R. McConnell, & M. A. McEvoy (Eds.), *Social competence of young children with disabilities: Issues and strategies for intervention* (pp. 307-320). Baltimore: Paul H. Brooks.

Harris, K. R., & Graham, S. (1994). Constructivism: Principles, paradigms, and integration. *Journal of Special Education, 28,* 233-247.

Hart, B. M. (1985). Naturalistic language training techniques. In S. F. Warren & A. K. Rogers-Warren (Eds.), *Teaching functional language* (pp. 63-88). Austin, TX: PRO-ED.

Hartup, W. W. (1992). Peer relations in early and middle childhood. In V. VanHasselt & M. Hersen (Eds.), *Handbook of social development* (pp. 257-281). New York: Plenum Press.

Hill, T. W. (1992). Reaching potential through appropriate assessment. In S. Bredekamp & T. Rosegrant (Eds.), *Reaching potentials: Appropriate curriculum and assessment for young children* (pp. 43-63). Washington, DC: National Association for the Education of Young Children.

Howes, C. (1987). Peer interaction of young children. *Monographs of the Society for Research in Child Development, 53* (1, Serial No. 217).

Isbell, R. (1995). *The complete learning center book.* Beltsville, MD: Gryphon House.

Kaiser, A. P., Yoder, P. J., & Keetz, A. (1992). Evaluating milieu teaching. In S. F. Warren & J. Reichle (Eds.), *Causes and effects in communication and language intervention* (pp. 9-47). Baltimore: Paul H. Brookes.

Kopp, C. B., Baker, B. L., & Brown, K. W. (1992). Social skills and their correlates: Preschoolers with developmental delays. *American Journal of Mental Retardation, 96,* 357-366.

Kostelnik, M. J., Doderman, A., & Whiren, A. (1993). *Developmentally appropriate programs in early childhood education.* New York: Macmillan.

Ladd, G. W., & Coleman, C. C. (1993). Young children's peer relationships: Forms, features, and functions. In B. Spodeck (Ed.), *Handbook of Research on the Education of Young Children* (pp. 57-76). New York: Macmillan.

Lieber, J., & Beckman, P. J. (1991). The role of toys in individual and dyadic play among young children with handicaps. *Journal of Applied Developmental Psychology, 12,* 189-203.

Mallory, B. L., & New, R. S. (1994). Social constructivist theory and principles of inclusion: Challenges for early childhood special education. *Journal of Special Education, 28,* 322-337.

McConnell, S. R., McEvoy, M. A., & Odom, S. L. (1992). Implementation of social competence interventions in early childhood special education classes: Current practices and future directions. In S. L. Odom, S. R. McConnell, & M. A. McEvoy (Eds.), *Social competence of young children with disabilities: Issues and strategies for intervention* (pp. 277-306). Baltimore: Paul H. Brookes.

McEvoy, M. A., Nordquist, V. M., Twardosz, S., Heckaman, K., Wehby, J. H., & Denny, R. K. (1988). Promoting autistic children's peer interaction in an integrated early childhood setting using affection activities. *Journal of Applied Behavior Analysis, 21,* 193-200.

McEvoy, M. A., & Odom, S. L. (1996). Strategies for promoting social interaction and emotional development of infants and young children with disabilities and their families. In S. L. Odom & M. McLean (Eds.), *Early intervention/Early childhood special education: Recommended practices* (pp. 223-244). Austin, TX: PRO-ED.

McEvoy, M. A., Odom, S. L., & McConnell, S. R. (1992). Peer social competence intervention for young children with disabilities. In S. L. Odom, S. R. McConnell, & M. A. McEvoy (Eds.), *Social competence of young children with disabilities: Issues and strategies for intervention* (pp. 113-134). Baltimore: Paul H. Brookes.

McEvoy, M. A., Shores, R. E., Wehby, J. H.,

Johnson, S. M., & Fox, J. J. (1990). Special education teachers implementation of procedures to promote social interaction among children in integrated settings. *Education and Training in Mental Retardation, 25,* 267-276.

McGee, G. G., Almeida, C., Sulzer-Azaroff, B., & Feldman, R. S. (1992). Promoting reciprocal interactions via peer incidental teaching. *Journal of Applied Behavior Analysis, 25,* 117-126.

McGee, G. G. (1995). *An Incidental Teaching Model for Toddlers with Autism.* Grant proposal, Early Education Program for Children with Disabilities, Office of Special Education Programs, U. S. Department of Education.

McLean, M. E., & Odom, S. L. (1996). Establishing recommended practices in early intervention/early childhood special education. In S. L. Odom & M. E. McLean (Eds.), *Early intervention/early childhood special education: Recommended practices* (pp. 1-22). Austin, TX: PRO-ED.

McMahon, R. J., & Forehand, R. (1988). Conduct disorders. In E. J. Mash & L. G. Terdal (Eds.), *Behavioral assessment of childhood disorders* (Second Edition, pp. 105-153). New York: Guilford.

Merrell, K. W. (1994). *Assessment of behavioral, social, and emotional problems: Direct and indirect methods for use with children and adolescents.* White Plains, NY: Longman.

Mize, J. (1995). Coaching preschool children in social skills: A cognitive-social learning curriculum. In G. Cartledge & J. F. Milburn (Eds.), *Teaching social skills to children and youth: Innovative approaches* (Third Edition) (pp. 237-261). Boston: Allyn and Bacon.

Mize, J., & Ladd, G. W. (1988). Predicting preschoolers' peer behavior and status from their interpersonal strategies: A comparison of hypothetical reflective and hypothetical enactive assessments. *Developmental Psychology, 24,* 782-788.

Mize, J., & Ladd, G. W. (1990). Toward the development of successful social skills training for preschool children. In S. R. Asher & J. D. Coie (Eds.). *Peer rejection in childhood* (pp. 338-361). New York: Cambridge University Press.

Mueller, E., & Silverman, N. (1989). Peer relations in maltreated children. In D. Cicchetti & V. Carlson (Eds.), *Child maltreatment: Theory and research on the causes and consequences of child abuse and neglect* (pp. 529-578). New York: Cambridge University Press.

National Association for the Education of Young Children, & National Association of Early Childhood Specialists in State Departments of Education. (1991). *Guidelines for appropriate curriculum content and assessment in program serving children ages 3 through 8.* Washington, DC: National Association for the Education of Young Children.

Nelson, K. (1981). Social cognition in a script framework. In J. H. Flavell & L. Ross (Eds.), *Children's thinking: What develops?* (pp. 338-361). Hillsdale, NJ: Erlbaum.

Noonan, M. J., & McCormick, L. (1993). *Early intervention in natural environments: Methods and procedures.* Pacific Grove, CA: Brooks/Cole Publishing.

Noonan, M. J., Ratokalau, N. B., Lauth-Torres, L., McCormick, L., Esaki, C. A., & Claybaugh, K. W. (1992). Validating critical skills for preschool success. *Infant-Toddler Intervention, 2,* 187-202.

Nordquist, V. M., Twardosz, S., & McEvoy, M. A. (1985, April). Promoting social interaction of autistic children through peer-mediated affection activities and incidental teaching. In *Current research in peer-mediated instruction for autistic and behavior disordered children.* Symposium conducted at the Annual Conference of The Council for Exceptional Children, Anaheim, California.

Nourot, P. M., & Van Hoorn, J. L. (1991). Symbolic play in preschool and primary settings. *Young Children, 46,* 40-50.

Odom, S. L., & Brown, W. H. (1993). Social interaction skills interventions for young children with disabilities in integrated settings. In C. A. Peck, S. L. Odom, & D. Bricker (Eds.), *Integrating young children* with disabilities into community programs: Ecological perspectives on research and implementation (pp. 39-64). Baltimore: Paul H. Brookes.

Odom, S. L., & McConnell, S. R. (1993). Play time/social time: Organizing your classroom to build interaction skills. Tucson, AZ: Communication Skill Builders.

Odom, S. L., McConnell, S. R., & Chandler, L. (1994). Acceptability, feasibility, and current use of social interaction interventions for preschool children with disabilities. *Exceptional Children, 60,* 226-237.

Odom, S. L., McConnell, S. R., & McEvoy, M. A. (1992). Peer-related social competence and its significance for young children with disabilities. In S. L. Odom, S. R. McConnell, & M. A. McEvoy (Eds.), *Social competence of young children with disabilities: Issues and strategies for intervention* (pp. 3-36). Baltimore: Paul H. Brookes.

Odom, S. L., & McEvoy, M. A. (1988). Integration of young children with handicaps and normally developing children. In S. Odom & M. Karnes (Eds.), *Early intervention for infants and children with handicaps: An empirical base* (pp. 241-267). Baltimore: Paul H. Brookes.

Odom, S. L., & Munson, L. (1996). Assessing social performance. In M. McLean, D. B. Bailey, & M. Wolery (Eds.), *Assessing infants and preschoolers with special needs* (pp. 398-434). Columbus, OH: Merrill.

Parker, J. G., & Asher, S. R. (1987). Peer relations and later personal adjustment: Are low-accepted children at risk? *Psychological Bulletin, 102,* 357-389.

Petrakos, H., & Howe, N. (1996). The influence of the physical design of the dramatic play center on children's play. *Early Childhood Research Quarterly, 11,* 63-77.

Piaget, J. (1926). *Language and thought in the child.* London: Kegan & Paul.

Richarz, S. (1993). Innovations in early childhood education: Models that support integration of children with varied developmental levels. In C. A. Peck, S. L. Odom, & D. Bricker (Eds.), *Integrating young children with disabilities into community programs: Ecological perspectives on research and implementation* (pp. 83-107). Baltimore: Paul H. Brookes.

Sainato, D. M., & Carta, J. J. (1992). Classroom influences on the development of social competence in young children with disabilities. In S. L. Odom, S. R. McConnell, & M. A. McEvoy (Eds.), *Social competence of young children with disabilities: Issues and strategies for intervention* (pp. 93-109). Baltimore: Paul H. Brookes.

Sainato, D. M., Goldstein, H., & Strain, P. S. (1992). Effects of self-evaluation on preschool children's use of social interactions strategies with their classmates with autism. *Journal of Applied Behavior Analysis, 25,* 127-141.

Schwartz, I. S., & Olswang, L. B. (1996). Evaluating child behavior change in natural settings: Exploring alternative strategies for data collection. *Topics in Early Childhood Special Education, 16,* 82-101.

Tremblay, A., Strain, P. S., Hendrickson, J. M., & Shores, R. E. (1981). Social interactions of normally developing preschool children: Using normative data for subject selection and target behavior selection. *Behavior Modification, 5,* 237-253.

Twardosz, S., Nordquist, V. M., Simon, R., & Botkin, D. (1983). The effects of group affection activities on the interaction of socially isolated children. *Analysis and Intervention in Developmental Disabilities, 3,* 311-338.

Vygotsky, L. S. (1978). *Mind and society: The development of higher psychological processes.* Cambridge, MA: Harvard University Press.

Wolery, M. (1996). Monitoring child progress. In M. McLean, D. B. Bailey, & M. Wolery (Eds.), *Assessing infants and preschoolers with special needs* (pp. 519-560). Columbus, OH: Merrill.

Wolery, M., Strain, P. S., & Bailey, D. B. (1992). Reaching potentials of children with special needs. In S. Bredekamp & T. Rosegrant (Eds.), *Reaching potentials: Appropriate curriculum and assessment for young children* (pp. 92-111). Washington, DC: National Association for the Education of Young Children.

Wolery, M., & Wilbers, J. (1994). *Including children with special needs in early childhood programs.* Washington, DC: National Association for the Education of Young Children.

Endnotes

[1] We use the term peer-related to indicate that we are particularly interested in young children's social interactions, social relationships, and social competence that is directly related to their social behavior with their peers.

[2] Recently, researchers have noted that children's peer-related social competence may be more complicated than previously thought (e.g., Hartup, 1992; Ladd & Coleman, 1993). On the one hand, children who have significant behavioral problems with peers (e.g., aggression, negative verbal interactions, property destruction) are at high risk for peer interaction and peer relation problems in early childhood as well as later psychopathology. On the other hand, children who are simply socially withdrawn from peers during early childhood, are not necessarily at significant risk for adolescent and adult social maladjustment. Nevertheless, young children who are significantly withdrawn do not have access to the same rich avenue their interactive peers have for acquiring important developmental abilities and are good candidates for peer-related social competence activities.

[3] It should be noted that the emergence of peer-related social competence is a developmental process for preschool children and because of individual differences young children will acquire peer-related social competencies at different points in time. Nevertheless, the acquisition of positive peer-related social competencies should be viewed as critical objectives for teachers who work with young children during the early childhood period.

[4] The proposed decision-making hierarchy is a revision of a previous hierarchy recommended by Odom and Brown (1993).

[5] Naturalistic teaching strategies are interventions that are implemented by teachers within the context of routine preschool activities. These teaching strategies are characterized by interventions that promote age-appropriate skills needed to participate in preschool settings for children without developmental delays. Naturalistic interventions are further characterized by teachers using methods that are only as complex and as intrusive as necessary to improve children's development while facilitating generalization and maintenance of newly acquired abilities [see Noonan & McCormick (1993) and Conroy & Brown (1997) for further discussion].

[6] We continue to recommend that teachers verify the children's frequency of peer interactions with periodic observations of the children of interest. Nevertheless, our experience has indicated that if children are not socially responsive during incidental teaching episodes that they frequently do not interact with peers during less structured circumstances.

[7] This table was included with permission from the Southern Early Childhood Association (SECA) and the authors of, "Suggestions for Enhancing the Social Behaviors of Preschoolers with Disabilities: Using Developmentally Appropriate Practices." The information appeared previously in an article in *Dimensions of Early Childhood* (Conroy, Langenbrunner, & Burleson, 1996).

CHAPTER 6

Assistive Technology and Preschool Children: Opening Doors

Ana Lòpez-De Fede
Department of Pediatrics
and The Institute for Families in Society
University of South Carolina

Janice Weber
Center for Developmental Disabilities
University of South Carolina

*"For most people, technology makes things easier.
For people with disabilities, technology makes things possible."*
Mary Pat Radabaugh (IBM National Support Center, 1989)

Dennis D. Durost and Sue L. Hutchinson

Technology changes the world in which we live and work. The word "technology" can bring to mind pictures of complicated equipment that is difficult to use. We sometimes forget that we use different types of technology in our routine activities. We use technology to help us every time the alarm clock signals a new day or we pick up the telephone. The remote control most people use to change television channels for convenience and ease can be an assistive technology device for someone with difficulty reaching for the tuning buttons on the television. Assistive technology allows the remote control to be adapted with scanning lights and a switch designed for the user. Thus, when the desired button lights up, the switch activates in any number of ways: with a head nod, an eye blink, a sound, or even a brain wave. The possibilities are endless with assistive technology.

Assistive technology offers great hope for individuals with developmental disabilities. For young children with developmental delays, assistive technology can be the means to move around in the home, to communicate with others, to be more independent, and to accomplish important developmental goals. These are just a few of the ways that technology can change the lives of young children.

Early childhood educators and parents of young children with developmental delays are often unaware of the role that assistive technology can play in helping children achieve their goals. The purpose of this chapter is to provide a resource for early childhood practitioners who struggle to find and incorporate assistive technology into the everyday lives of young children with developmental delays. We will focus on the benefits of using assistive technology with young children and explore the resources available to educators and families who want to ensure full participation of young children with developmental delays.

Legislative History: The Right To Assistive Technology

The legislative history of assistive technology is divided into two basic categories of federal public law those that influence the educational setting of young children with developmental delays and those that influence the technological services.

Public laws with the greatest impact on addressing the needs of young children with developmental delays include: (a) *Section 504 of the Vocational Rehabilitation Act (PL 93-112) Amendments, 1973*; (b) *Education of the Handicapped Act (PL 94-142), 1975 and its 1986 (PL 99-457), 1990 (PL 101-476), 1997 PL 105-17 amendments*; (c) *Technology Related Assistance for Individuals with Developmental Delays Act (PL 100-407), 1988*; and (d) *ADA, Americans with Disabilities Act (PL 101-336), 1990*. All four of these laws influence either the services that young children with developmental delays receive, their educational setting, or both.

Vocational Rehabilitation Act, 1973. Section 504 of PL 93-112 of the Vocational Rehabilitation Act is a basic civil rights provision for individuals with developmental delays. It states "No otherwise qualified handicapped individual in the United States shall, solely by reason of his handicap, be excluded from the participation in, be denied the benefits of, or be subjected to discrimination under any program actively receiving federal assistance" *(PL 93-112, Section 504.33)*. Section 504 provides the legal foundation for protecting students with physical developmental delays who do not qualify for special educational services. Its importance for young children with developmental delays is to mandate that programs make special arrangements to provide access to the full range of programs and activities for all students. This includes children being provided services in childcare centers that receive federal funding.

Children with severe disabilities participating in early childhood programs for whom assistive technology could increase their level of independence may be eligible to receive funding for assistive devices under the *Vocational Rehabilitation Act*. Information on specific services available to young children with developmental delays and their eligibility criteria can be obtained by contacting your State Rehabilitation Agency or the University Affiliated Program in your State.

Education of the Handicapped Act, 1975. The Education for All Handicapped Children Act, PL 94-142 (referred to as *Education for the Handicapped Act*) passed in 1975, guarantees the right to a free and appropriate public education for all children. Subsequent amendments in 1986, 1990, and 1997 expand the rights to all children and youth with disabilities and ensure the rights of their parents or guardians to be active participants in the development of individual educational and services plans.[1]

The *1986 Amendments to EHA, Preschool (Part B)* and *Infant/Toddler (Part H) Programs* require that states provide special education and related services to children from 3 to 5 years of age. It also establishes a new, voluntary state program for providing early intervention services for infants and toddlers (birth to two years of age) with developmental delays and their families. This amendment significantly expands the rights and entitlement of young children with developmental delays. Part H services mandate a comprehensive multidisciplinary evaluation and Individual Family Service Plan (IFSP). Among the key components are the rights of children to be educated in the Least Restrictive Environment and parents rights to Due Process in the provision of services.

The 1990 amendments to EHA changed the title of the law to *the Individuals with Developmental Disabilities Education Act (IDEA), PL 101-476*. It added two new provisions to be included in the development of individual educational plans, assistive technology and transition services. IDEA makes it possible for states and localities to receive federal funds to assist in the education of infants, toddlers, preschoolers, children, and youth with disabilities. States must fully comply with all the administrative regulations under this law to remain eligible for federal funds. States and localities have the right to establish eligibility criteria under IDEA, therefore, programs and services across the country are very diverse in nature. One of the key provisions of IDEA is the mandate which affects the placement of children with developmental delays. The spirit of the law is for young children with disabilities to be educated with peers who are not disabled. It challenges service providers to find creative ways to implement this law and increases local resources for providing services.

IDEA establishes the mandate to provide assistive devices to young children with disabilities for whom the need for assistive technology is part of the Individualized Family Services Plan (IFSP) or their Individualized Educational Plan (IEP). Thus, if assistive technology is necessary for the young child with disabilities to receive a Free and Appropriate Public Education (FAPE) or it is included as part of the IFSP or IEP, the local education (LEA) must make the assistive devices available in the preschool classroom or the child care center serving the young child. An excellent resource entitled *Technology and the Individualized Education Program* is available from the RESNA Technical Assistance Project (1992) (Phone: 202-857-1140 Voice/TDD).

Technology Related Assistance For Individuals With Developmental Disabilities Act, 1988. The enactment of *PL 100-407, the Technology Related Assistance for Individuals Act of 1988 ("Tech Act")*, reauthorized in 1994 as *PL 103-218*, provides funds for states to develop and promote the use of assistive technology. States receiving funds may develop or conduct the following activities: (a) model delivery systems; (b) state-wide needs assessment; (c) support groups; (d) public awareness programs; (e) training and technical assistance; (f) access to information; (g) interagency agreements; and (h) other activities necessary for developing, implementing, or evaluating state-wide service delivery systems.

The impact of the *Technology Related Assistance for Individuals with Developmental Disabilities Act* can be measured through four important system change strategies:

1. The emphasis is on the individual first and not the disability. The Tech Act changed the language of legislation from the handicapped to individuals with developmental disabilities, providing the framework for language that has influenced all legislative mandates after its inception;

2. The incorporation of assistive technology services and devices as essential program components serving individuals with developmental disabilities;

3. Involvement of consumers and care givers in the decision making positions with organizations serving individuals with developmental disabilities; and

4. System change mandates to foster partnerships between State agencies serving individuals with developmental disabilities.

The terms assistive technology devices and services definitions were first defined in this legislation. Tech Act programs can be a valuable resource for early childhood programs on the funding and availability of assistive technology services available through public and private sources within their state. Information on funded state projects can be obtained by calling the RESNA Technical Assistance Project (Phone 202:-857-1140 Voice/TDD).

Americans with Disabilities Act, 1990. The *Americans with Disabilities Act (ADA)* ensures the full civil rights of all individuals with disabilities. It guarantees equal opportunity and reasonable accommodations for individuals with disabilities in employment, public accommodation, transportation, state and local government services, and telecommunications. Thus, providing a reasonable accommodation may involve the acquisition or modification of equipment or devices [*PL 101-336, Section 1630.2 (n)*].

The ADA emphasizes that reasonable accommodations must be afforded to an individual both during the application process as well as once the person has been hired. Assistive technology can be one important means of providing these accommodations. It ensures young children with developmental delays access to services throughout their lifetime. The assurance of full access of young children with developmental disabilities will only become a reality with the introduction of assistive technology at the *earliest* possible educational experience of the young child (e.g., child care centers, preschools, Head Start Programs).

Defining Assistive Technology Devices And Services

Recent legislative history provides a clear legal mandate for the incorporation of assistive technology services and devices into everyday life. However, it is the needs young children with developmental delays have that provide the impetus for practitioners and care givers to employ assistive technology in early childhood programs. For example, parents have commented upon their children's new sense of mastery over their environment and increased self esteem when assistive technology is employed. In addition, they report that experiences with microcomputers provide their children with a breadth of opportunities for advancing cognitive, language, and social skills. One parent aptly summarized her thoughts about the early introduction of the computer to her young son with developmental delays:

> The computer has meant hours of fun and success for our son Ryan. He can draw, type his name, play games, learn strategies, and zap things whenever he gets the urge. And even more than that, he can play with other kids, be the leader, and be the teacher if there is a computer around . . . the computer has shown us his spirit, and shown others that a neat person lies within that little blond, half-blind, non-verbal five year old wheelchair user (Callison & Howard, 1982, p. 10).

Thus, assistive technology devices, and the technical assistance services that support the use of those devices with children are the *keys* that unlock doors that have been closed to children with developmental delays.

What is assistive technology? Assistive technology can be any device, item, or piece of equipment that increases, maintains, or improves the quality of life of young children with developmental delays. Assistive technology can include eating utensils, adapted toys, computers, seating systems, powered mobility equipment, augmentative communication devices, and switches. In other words, assistive technology includes the entire range of human inventions from modified simple spoons for eating, to complex computer systems that "speak" for an individual without speech. Assistive technology is a means rather than an end, however. For example, an adaptive switch that starts a toy is a means to more sophisticated and independent play. Touching a computer screen to create sounds and colors can help children gain an understanding of the effect their actions on the world. Pointing to pictures can be a way for children with communication difficulties to interact within their families and peers.

Assistive technology can offer exciting ways for children to explore their environment, tell stories, and learn new things — things all children like to do! Young children with developmental delays do not always need expensive and complicated items to help them in their daily lives. The goal is *not* to equip the child with the most technologically advanced device, rather, it is to provide the child with the device that best meets his need for independence and inclusion in early childhood settings. Assistive devices or *adaptive devices* are commonly classified into two major categories: *high-technology* and *low-technology*. "Low-tech" devices can be purchased at a hardware store, selected from a catalog, or fabricated using tools and materials that can be found in many well-equipped home workshops (Franklin, 1991). On the other hand, "high-tech" devices frequently incorporate some type of computer chip; such as the "talking clock," a computer, or an augmentative communication device (Franklin, 1991). Many high-tech devices such as motorized wheelchairs or computers can be expensive and complicated to operate; however, many low-tech devices are inexpensive and easy to use. For example, the use of tape recorders to help children practice speech, or the use of large tweezers as a dressing aide to help open and close zippers, are inexpensive low-tech devices that benefit young children with developmental delays. Table 1 illustrates examples of "high" and "low" technology applications in early childhood programs.

Assistive technology devices can enable children with developmental delays to be educated in less restrictive environments by providing them with critical support needed to participate in early childhood programs. Seating aids may help position children with physical impairments to improve their attention to and participation in early childhood curricular activities. Mobility aids can help children significant cerebral palsy to travel about and move around within programs. Augmentative communication devices help children with communication disorders interact with others and increase children's social contact. Computer software can provide instructional support and much needed practice for children with developmental delays in basic preacademic skills. Sensory support devices can enhance the development of children with sensory impairments through visual and auditory aids that promote their participation in activities. Recreational aids may help children with developmental delays have fun with peers

Cassette recorder	Computer voice recognition software
Student workbook	Computer instructional software
Picture board	Augmentative communications devices
Taped Instructions	Speech synthesizers
Simple switches	Head pointers
Simple keyboard	Alternative keyboards (e.g., Power Pad, Intellikeys)

Table 1. Examples of Low-Tech and High-Tech Devices

while maintaining their physical fitness. Self-care aids help students with developmental delays take care of personal needs during the day. In short, assistive technology devices are any pieces of equipment or product systems whether acquired off the shelf, modified or customized that are used to increase, maintain, or improve functional capabilities of individuals with developmental delays [*PL 100-407* codified as *20 U.S.C., Section 1401(25)*]. A glossary of common assistive technology terms can be found at the conclusion of this chapter as a guide and reference for the reader.

What are assistive technology services? Assistive technology is much more than equipment. Assistive technology includes both appropriate assessment and effective intervention services. Successful use of assistive technology requires careful assessment to identify appropriate solutions for young children with developmental delays. Assistive technology services include "...services that directly assist an individual with a disability in the selection, acquisition, or use of an assistive technology device" [*PL 100-407 codified as 20 U.S.C., Section 1402 (26)*]. Services can include evaluation and assessment, training, consultation, purchasing and leasing of devices, equipment demonstration and loan, resource lending libraries, advocacy, and information and referral for further assistance when necessary.

Federal laws may require that assistive technology services and devices be provided to children with disabilities by an agency designated as the state lead agency for assistive technology. The process of receiving assistive technology services will require families and professionals to work together as collaborators to develop children's Individualized Educational Plan (IEP) or Individualized Family Service Plans (IFSP). Individualized plans will often include goals for learning and independence that can only be met by using appropriate assistive devices. A component of any IEP or IFSP requiring assistive devices should be the services necessary to assess needs and select and use devices appropriately.

Assistive technology can help young children with developmental delays to participate more fully in daily activities. It is a means through which children can become more independent and meet their full developmental potential. Given the potential benefits of assistive technology, it is imperative that educators and care givers consider making it an integral part of all plans developed for young children with developmental delays. However, it is not always clear which state agency or program is responsible for ensuring that young children with developmental delays have access to assistive technology. The Office of Special Education Programs (OSEP) clarified the rights of children with disabilities to assistive technology devices and services under *PL 94-142*. OSEP regulations have clearly indicated that:

➡ school districts cannot presumptively deny assistive technology to a student with a disability;

➡ the need for assistive technology should be considered on an individual case-by-case basis in the development of the students Individual Education Program (IEP);

➡ assistive technology can be special education or related services; assistive technology can also be a form of supplementary aid or service utilized to facilitate a child's education in a regular education environment; and

➡ if participants on the IEP team determine a child requires assistive technology in order to receive a free appropriate education, and designate such assistive technology as either special education or a related service, then the services must be provided at *no cost* to the parents (Office of Special Education Programs, 1990)

How does this apply to youngsters in inclusive preschool programs? The determination of whether individual children will benefit from assistive technology should be based on an appropriate technology assessment. Once the need for assistive technology is determined there is a mandate for preschool programs receiving federal funds to provide assistive technology devices and services to young children with developmental delays at **no cost** to parents.

Technology Assessments With Young Children

Appropriate assessment is critical to match children's needs and capabilities with the right devices and services. During comprehensive assessments, professionals gather and interpret information that may include medical, educational, and family histories. The assessment for and selection and acquisition of assistive devices is a process that requires parents and staff members in preschool programs to work as partners with trained assistive technology professionals. This partnership starts with a common understanding of the type of technology assessment needed by children and specific action steps necessary to complete the assessment process.

The assessment process. The assistive technology decision-making process includes a variety of action steps designed to ensure that the needs of young children with developmental delays are met. Early childhood personnel should be an integral part of this assessment process if the assistive technology needs of the child are to be meet. These action steps include, but, are not limited to the following:

1. Use a team approach: When assistive technology decisions are made by a team of professionals, parents, early childhood educators and other interested individuals, there is more assurance that an appropriate choice will be made and provide stronger justification for securing funds. A proper assessment team should be identified and assembled. Family involvement is crucial, as is the input of anyone who spends significant time with the child on a consistent basis. The knowledge of the care givers of the young child developmental delays can allow preschool and child care center staff members to serve as a vital link between the assessment team and the care giver.

2. Gather information and documentation: Prior assessments may contain much of the background information needed, such as medical diagnosis, family history, therapist assessment, and educational records. If not, the necessary information needs to be gathered. It is also important for team members to observe children in a variety of environments (e.g., home, school, and community) and record day-to-day activities in each environment. Observing children in multiple settings identifies natural abilities and

preferences and helps determine needs and goals. Documentation should continue throughout the assessment process. For example, specific concerns and questions to be addressed during assessment should be written and shared with the assessment team. Any concerns and questions will help to determine the type of assessments to be administered and the goals of the assessment process. Knowledge of the child and her home environment can help to facilitate the assessment process and avoid dupli-

Education	Determines the placement and plan for a child referred for special education. Assistive technology needs may be identified from information collected during an educational assessment.
Mobility	Determines the placement and plan for a child referred for special education. Assistive technology needs may be identified from information collected during an educational assessment. Assessment looks at the abilities of and necessary skills needed by young children to move as independently as possible.
Seating/positioning	Fits a seating system to best suit a child's shape or posture. Proper positioning is necessary when deciding how a child will best access a computer or communication device. Proper seating/positioning can make the most of the child's physical capabilities, minimize fatigue, and prevent skin breakdown caused by pressure sores.
Communication	Can be one of the most complex in terms of assistive technology because it includes speaking, hearing, reading, and writing. Communication devices range from no technology to computers with speech output which can also perform the usual functions.
Computer access	Determines the best input device or method of access and should also address software and training needs. For example, switch access is often the alternate choice to a keyboard for operating a computer; communication device; or other equipment, such as environmental controls. This assessment determines which of the many possible switches will be most effective in conjunction with the position that will work best with the individual child.
Environment	May be needed to determine the choice of aids for daily living functions, including home modification, to determine an appropriate modification to the environment.

Table 2: Technology- Related Assessments

cation of efforts and wasted time. Early childhood educators who work with young children with developmental delays can be the most important source of information for the assessment team on the most appropriate type of assessment needed given the child's home environment, disability, current use of assistive devices, and the preschool environment.

3. Conduct the appropriate type of assessment: Various types of assessments are commonly used to determine the technology needs of young children with developmental delays. The choice of the type of assessment should be firmly grounded in the information needed to properly meet the technology needs of *individual* children. The most common types of assessments are shown in Table 2. The assessment results can be used to identify the most appropriate technology-related needs for *individual* children.

4. Identify preferences, needs, and abilities and set goals: The identification of preferences and interests, capabilities and needs is pivotal to goal-setting in the assistive technology decision-making process. Because most devices will be used on a daily basis, personal preference and motivation are strong factors in whether the intervention is successful. Teachers in preschool programs will have first hand knowledge on the motivational level and interests of the child ensuring a more appropriate "fit" between the technology and the child. This can reduce the anxiety and frustration levels of the child during the initial adjustment period to the with the new assistive devices.

5. Prepare the environment for technology: The environment should be prepared *both* during and after the assessment process for subsequent use of assistive devices by children. This requires a team determination about which environments may need adapting to ensure maximum access and safety for children. A trial period may be necessary and extremely helpful when evaluating the appropriateness of any environmental modifications. In preparing the environment, an important component that should be considered is the development of plans to train early childhood personnel to help the child use the recommended assistive device(s). Preschool teachers have an obligation to make sure that they feel comfortable in their knowledge of the workings of the assistive devices and their potential use in their program.

6. Match devices to individual children: The functional abilities of children should be matched with characteristics of devices. This requires the direct participation of early childhood educators with individuals who are knowledgeable about assistive technology and *jointly* can suggest devices that match the needs of children with developmental delays.

7. Conduct assistive technology trial periods: An essential action step is the establishment of a trial period that provides children with opportunities to borrow and use potential assistive devices. Trial periods provide valuable information about the applicability of devices within the child's environment. Also, a trial period allows for evaluating children's adjustment to the

assistive devices. It is an essential step prior to purchasing equipment for children. Tech Act and state Vocational Rehabilitation agencies can be a valuable resource in helping early childhood program staff to locate assistive technology loaner program's to facilitate this trial period.

The technology assessment process should be documented in a summary report of findings and proposed solutions. The report should include the primary goals of the assessment, what was learned by the assessment and trial period, how the use of the device will be implemented, how to maintain the device, training issues, and time lines for follow-up evaluations. Proper documentation of the entire assessment process can ensure that the necessary support services and funding sources are secured to assist children with developmental delays and their families. It also eliminates unwarranted repetition and duplication efforts.

Integrating Assistive Technology Into Inclusive Classrooms

A great deal has been accomplished in the past 20 years, particularly with respect to providing a free, appropriate education for children with developmental delays (Heward & Orlansky, 1992). The proportion of children and adults served in residential facilities and separate schools has declined dramatically, and the placement of students in general education classes in public schools is increasing annually. Approximately 73% of students requiring special education services are served in general education classrooms for part (i.e., 40% or more for part of the school day) or all of the school day (U. S. Department of Education, 1996).

Keeping pace with the debate and changing educational practices and services for students with disabilities is a challenge for educators, families, and service providers. These changes, coupled with the rapid growth and benefits of assistive technology for young children with developmental delays, make the inclusion debate in many cases a moot point. Basically, assistive technology "levels the playing field" for all young children with developmental delays and allows them to be educated in the most inclusive environment. Thus, the issue is no longer should inclusion be a reality for all students but rather, how to define inclusion to reflect the spirit and implementation of the law. Inclusion for preschoolers with developmental delays increases their social competence, and they spend more time playing and interacting positively with peers (Odom & Brown, 1993; Brown, Horn, Heiser, & Odom, in press). Inclusion also appears to have positive effects on other behaviors such as, improved sophistication of play. However, for many children without the use of assistive technology devices and services it would be impossible for them to be educated in inclusive preschool environments. Assistive technology devices and services should be a critical component of every inclusive preschool and child care center program. The next section of this chapter explore some key strategies for overcoming barriers to the use of assistive technology in early childhood programs.

Strategies for overcoming barriers to using assistive technology. The benefits of assistive technology cannot be realized by young children with developmental delays unless early childhood educators are adequately prepared to operate the assistive devices and integrate them into their daily routine. Barriers commonly associated with the use of assistive technology in educational settings range from lack of familiarity and training with assistive devices, limited portability of the equipment, to the unavailability of support mechanisms that encourage the use of assistive devices (McGregor & Pachuski, 1996). It is only through the involvement of early childhood teachers as equal partners in the integration of technology in early childhood settings that effective strategies can be implemented to overcome barriers to the use of technology. In order to achieve this goal, early childhood personnel should strive to incorporate the following practices:

1. Provide information to staff members on successful technology and inclusion practices. This will allow staff members to make informed decisions about the use of technology and whether with the use of technology inclusion is the best educational approach for children in their programs.

2. Learn about the law and recent court cases. Inclusion is not something a child should earn, it is a child's right. The involvement of family members with programs serving their children can help to ensure that barriers restricting funding and equal access are minimized. The school system has a legal obligation to provide the least restrictive program if it is requested. Children cannot be placed in more restrictive settings unless a school system can demonstrate that, even with the provision of necessary support services and supplementary aids; inclusive settings are not appropriate in meeting the needs of these students.

3. The involvement of early childhood educators in the technology assessment process is a powerful tool to ensure that the children's programs provide all the necessary support services and supplementary aids. Staff members who are actively involved and knowledgeable about the technology needs of children in their programs can provide the appropriate level of assistance for children who are adapting to using assistive devices. Early childhood educators can support schools and districts in developing high-quality inclusion programs. Successful inclusion programs are ones which have been developed carefully, with input from everyone who will be involved—administrators, teachers, families, and students.

4. Develop support groups and mechanisms within the school for staff members who work with children using assistive devices. The exchange of information and the development of appropriate support mechanism provide early childhood educators with the necessary tools to overcome barriers to the use of technology.

Technology applications for early childhood classrooms. The use of assistive technology with young children requires that the "IN words" guide our program activities:
- Inclusion
- Integration
- Interaction
- Involvement

Important considerations for integrating technology applications include:

1. Goal Setting: What skills need to be enhanced? Goals may be in any one of several areas of development: cognitive, motor, social and self help, communication. Even toys with switches should be used with a purpose in mind, especially with children with severe disabilities.

2. Positioning: Children and equipment should be correctly positioned. Occupational and physical therapists should be involved in decisions about positioning and the types of input devices and methods to use.

3. Activity Design: Think about activities already being conducted in programs and classrooms to reinforce the technology goals of children.

4. Simple to Complex: Use devices that are simple, not intrusive, and not likely to need repair.

5. Patience: Understand that you may need to wait for responses from children. There is often an adjustment and reaction period for children before they become interested and motivated to use devices.

6. Reinforcement: Adults as well as children outgrow interest in materials, over time, and participation may require new reinforcement techniques as well as novel toys or materials.

7. Other factors: Always remember that a child's response to a device or adaptation may be affected by his temperment, the time of day, and the presence of environmental distractions.

8. Creativity: Be creative and never be afraid to use a device or a certain piece of software because it looks too hard for individual children.

8. Finally: Keep in mind that it is the process not the product that determines the success of technology applications.

Table 3 provides an illustration of technology applications for use in the early childhood classroom to help children meet their goals. A glossary of common assistive technology terms can be found at the conclusion of this chapter as guide and reference for the reader. In the next section we will explore assistive technology service delivery approaches with young children with developmental delays.

Service Delivery Approaches

Service delivery approaches designed to meet the needs of young children with developmental delays take two distinct formats, the expansion of traditional service delivery programs, and the development of innovative, non-traditional service delivery models. Not all approaches or programs are highlighted in this section; rather a selection of approaches and strategies that more closely demonstrate the current state of practice.

Innovative programs and services. Successful inclusion of young children with developmental delays can often be achieved with information, training, and consultation available to early childhood professionals. An example of a project designed to address technical assistive needs is Project Enhancement that was developed under the auspices of the South Carolina University Affiliated Program. The first author served as the principal

Application	Goals	Equipment examples	Examples of classroom considerations
Positioning	Increased functioning and participation through stable and comfortable positioning	Sidelying frames; walkers; crawling assists; floor sitters; chair inserts; standing aids; etc.	Positioning considerations should include student's position in relation to peers and teacher
Access	Enhancement of speed, accuracy, endurance and independence	Input devices (switch, expanded keyboard, mouse, touch window; and speech recognition); head pointers; keyboard emulators; electronic communication	Access technologies are keys to effective and efficient use of devices. Integration of systems (powered mobility, computer access, and environmental controls) to maximize independence
Environmental control	Positive control of the environment without assistance from care givers	Switch connections for battery operated items; remote control units	Introduced initially in infant programs; control units can eliminate wires and optimize use of assistive devices
Augmentative communication	Independent means of expression (writing, speaking, drawing)	Symbol communication boards and devices, speech synthesizers, recorded speech devices, and communication enhancement software	Intervention begins with setting up the classroom for communication. Group call signals, communication boards projected on overheads, language master cards with messages and symbols, and speech output devices can all be used to enhance communication
Visual aids	Enhancement or interpretation of visual information	Screen readers, screen enlargers, Braille light boxes, high contrast materials and synthesizers	Vision is a major learning mode. It is often difficult to determine how best to enhance the vision of children who can not describe what they see or perceive. Monitor responses to technology carefully with each device

Table 3: Assistive Technologies In The Early Childhood Classroom

Application	Goals	Equipment examples	Examples of classroom considerations
Mobility	Independent movement, exploration, social interaction, and learning	Self-propelled (walkers) or powered recreational (bikes and scooters) and mobility aids (wheelchairs)	Mobility aids are effective socialization, communication, and environmental controls. Do not rule out powered mobility. Children as young as 15 months can use electronic wheelchairs with supervision
Recreation, leisure	Access to materials, activities allowing peer interaction, hobby development and use of free time	Outdoor adaptations (slides, swings), computer games, play materials (indoor/outdoor carpets on trays), Velcro on toys	Listening and viewing activities (music and tapes, slide/tape show) dramatic play (voice output communication aids), adapted puzzles
Self care	Independent self-care activities	Electric feeders, adapted utensils (built-up spoons, scoop dish), toilet seats, aids for tooth brushing and grooming	Incorporate self care and adaptation as they occur naturally in activities of feeding, dressing (coats, shoes), toileting, meal preparation

Note: Adapted from Blackstone, S. (1990). Augmentative Communication News, 3(6), 3. Reproduced with publisher's permission.

Table 3: Assistive Technologies In The Early Childhood Classroom (cont.)

investigator on the development of a multimedia, self-directed curriculum on the benefits and uses of assistive technology applications with young children. The multimedia computer training curriculum exposes early interventionists to the world of assistive technology and provides critical information about common assistive devices in use by young children with developmental delays. The information provides professionals with access to local and national resources. Comprised of four modules covering assistive devices for aids for daily living devices, communication, mobility and computer access, the self-directed modules allows users to add information on any of devices and to print the materials for easy dissemination. The curriculum is a part of a comprehensive training initiative funded by the Administration on Developmental Disabilities of the Administration for Children and Families.

In another project, increased access to assistive technology devices is the goal of the Kentucky Early Intervention Systems (KEIS). KEIS helps personnel at 15 Points of Entry (POE) sites in the state to develop policies and procedures for assistive technology services for young children with developmental delays. In collaboration with personnel at the State Tech Act project, the Kentucky Assistive Technology Service Network, the project personnel provides training, tracking, monitoring, and loaning of equipment and toys to consumers. Each POE is provided a kit of equipment with the training and technical assistance necessary to match the appropriate assistive device to the needs of young children with developmental delays. The strength of this project lies in its ability to build on interagency collaboration to address the needs of consumers for access to assistive devices in their local communities.

The Computer Equipment Recycling and Exchange Program of The United Cerebral Palsy Associations, Inc. (UCPA), is an initiative program through which UCPA solicits donations of computer equipment and assistive devices from public and private sources. This program provides the mechanism through which young children with developmental delays and their families can borrow and "try out" needed devices prior to purchase. UCPA also makes available to consumers purchased devices that are no longer needed by previous users. This UCPA recycling program is one that can be instituted at the school district level or within early childhood programs to ensure the availability of devices for children in both classroom and home settings.

PennTECH Assistive Technology Early Intervention Program provides a range of services for children birth through 3 years of age. Services include a short-term loan program, training, consultation, and model early childhood technology sites located throughout Pennsylvania. All services are available to family members, educators, and therapists associated with young children. Among the innovative features of this program is co-location of sites within established child development centers providing a working model of childhood inclusion which is aided by assistive technology.

Since 1975, personnel with the Macomb Projects within the Department of Elementary Education at Western Illinois University have worked with young children with developmental delays and computer technology. Project staff have developed software, hardware, and peripheral adaptations to meet the goals of young children with developmental delays. Project ACCT: Activating Children through Technology is an early childhood innovative microcomputer curriculum model developed as part of the Macomb Projects. The curriculum is a comprehensive competency-based program designed to help early childhood educators integrate computers as a tool in early childhood programs.

The mission of the National Center to Improve Practice (NCIP) is to improve educational outcomes for students with delays by promoting the effective use of assistive and instructional technologies among educators. NCIP offers a series of video profiles which illustrate how students with delays use a range of assistive and instructional technologies to improve their learning. Of special interest to early childhood educators is the video "Welcome to My Preschool! Communicating with Technology." This 14-minute video and its accompanying materials are designed to explore the use of high- and low-technology tools in an integrated preschool classroom (National Center to Improve Practice, 1994).

In summary, the programs reviewed are innovative because of their outreach efforts, interagency collaboration, and creativity in meeting the needs of early childhood educators and parents of young children with developmental delays. These programs all address the challenge to move assistive technology service delivery systems from the impersonal "Their" project to the personal "Our" assistive technology program. The almost daily technological advances require early childhood educators to form partnerships with personnel in programs serving children with developmental delays. It is only thorough these professional partnerships that the possibilities of assistive technology will be realized for all young children with developmental delays. Without assistive technology the keys that can unlock the world for children with developmental delays to countless of new possibilities may never be turned.

Conclusions

Assistive Technology offers great hope for young children with developmental delays. Young children with developmental delays are at special risk for problems in early childhood programs. Yet the impact of the disability can be diminished through the timely and thoughtful use of assistive devices, instructional materials, and technical assistance services in preschool classrooms. Assistive technology devices and services can ensure that children with developmental delays have opportunities to achieve their potential by ensuring supportive environments and adequate resources to meet their developmental needs.

The right to assistive technology and services is relatively new movement for young children with delays, starting in 1973 with the passage of *Section 504 of the Vocational Rehabilitation Act Amendments* and culminating in 1990 with the *American with Disabilities Act*. Laws with the greatest influence on enhancing access to technology-related services and educational settings for young children with are:

➡ *Section 504 of the Vocational Rehabilitation Act*;

➡ *Education of the Handicapped Act* and its amendments;

➡ *Technology Related Assistance for Individuals with Disabilities Act*; and

➡ *the Americans with Disabilities Act*.

These laws stand at the forefront of an "assistive technology revolution" that supports and enhances the daily lives of young children with delays.

Early childhood educators face a number of challenges in ensuring that assistive technology devices and services are appropriate to meet the needs of young children with developmental delays. For example, how can early childhood educators determine which is the most appropriate technology assessment? What safeguards should be incorporated into the technology assessment process to facilitate the learning environments of young children with developmental delays? What strategies can be used to build an inclusive preschool program? What is the role of family members in the determination of assistive technology goals for children with developmental delays? It is hoped this chapter provides practical information and strategies that will help early childhood educators begin addressing these critical challenges. Assistive technology is not a panacea, but it can help children to realize their human potential. Assistive technology can help young children with developmental delays define their participation preschool programs by their abilities rather than their limitations.

Preparation of this chapter was partially supported by Grant 90-DD-0308 from the Administration on Developmental Disabilities, Administration on Youth and Families, U.S. Department of Health and Human Services.

Assistive Technology Resources

The following listing may be used as a resource for locating specific national organizations, information networks, referral centers, and publications that provide information on assistive technology. This listing is by no means complete, as there are many local and community organizations that provide the same information. Inclusion of any resource in this listing does not indicate an endorsement.

Goodwill Industries of America, Inc.
9200 Wisconsin Ave., Bethesda, MD 20814, 301-530-6500

National Easter Seal Society
70 E. Lake St., Chicago, IL. 60601, 800-221-6827

National Information Center for Children and Youth with Disabilities
P.O. Box 1492, Washington, DC 20013, 800-999-5599

National Institute on Disability and Rehabilitation Research (NIDRR)
U.S. Dept. of Education, 400 Maryland Ave. S.W., Washington, DC 20202, 202-732-1134

National Rehabilitation Association
633 S. Washington St., Alexandria, VA 22314, 703-836-0850

National Rehabilitation Information Center (NARIC)
8455 Colesville Rd. – Suite 935, Silver Springs, MD 20910-3319, 800-346-2742

Trace R&D Center
S-151 Waisman Center, 1500 Highland Ave., Madison, WI 53705, 608-262-6966

United Cerebral Palsy Association
1522 K St., NW, Suite 1112, Washington, DC 20005, 800-872-5827

World Institute on Disability
510 16th St., Suite 100, Oakland, CA 94612, 510-763-41009

Glossary of Common Assistive Technology Terms

ADA (Americans with Disabilities Act) A federal law which extends to all Americans with disabilities civil rights and legal protections in housing, employment, education and use of public social, recreational, and transportation facilities.

ADL (Activities of Daily Living) Daily self-care activities including, dressing, bathing, toileting, and eating.

Augmentative Communication Devices Systems of adapted technology which encourage and enhance verbal and non-verbal communication. The type and complexity of the assistive device is determined by the physical, cognitive, and social needs of the child.

Assessment Process A series of test and observations that determines the child's strength's and weaknesses used to determine the need for assistive technology.

Assistive Technology Device Any piece of equipment or product system, whether acquired commercially off the shelf, modified or customized, that are used to increase, maintain, or improve the functional abilities of individuals with disabilities. Assistive technology devices can be refer to as adaptive devices or durable medical equipment when purchased through health insurance policies or programs.

Assistive Technology Services Any service that assists an individual with disability in the selection, acquisition, or use of an assistive technology device.

High-Tech Device Devices that frequently incorporate some type of computer chip; such as the "talking clock", a computer, or an augmentative communication device.

IDEA (Individuals with Disabilities Act) The federal law originally passed by Congress in 1975 as the *Education of All Handicapped Children Act, P.L. 94-142*. Establishes the legal right of all children to appropriate public education in the least restrictive environment possible.

IEP (Individualized Education Plan An educational process document designed by a team consisting of parents, educators, administrators, and related personnel. This document states the strengths and needs of and individual student, and goals and objectives for one school year for students 3-21 years old.

IFSP (Individual Family Service Plan) A process document used in programs for infants and toddlers 0-3 years old to establish and organize goals and objectives for a team of professionals working with families of children at risk for or having developmental problems.

Low-Tech Device Devices that can be purchased at a hardware store, selected from a catalog, or fabricated using tools and materials that can be found in many well-equipped home workshops.

Orthotic Device Braces or mobility equipment (wheelchair, walker, prone stander) which give support to muscles and joints to encourage or support independent movement.

Sensory Support Devices Enhance children's development through visual and auditory aids that promote their participation in activities.

Speech Recognition Systems The goal of speech recognition systems is for the computer to recognize continuous human speech and to act on spoken commands.

Switching Systems A switch is a device similar to a light switch – it is either open or closed controlling the flow of electricity. Children with disabilities can use switches to operate computers, toys and communication devices.

References

Alliance for Technology Access. (1995). Real people, real technology, real solutions. Adaptive technology for the handicapped. *Exceptional Parent, 25*(11), 30.

Blackstone, S. (1990). Technology applications. *Augmentative Communication News, 3*(6), 3.

Brown, W. H., Horn, E. M., Heiser, J. G., & Odom, S. L. (in press). Project BLEND: An inclusive model for early intervention services. *Journal of Early Intervention*.

Callison, P., & Howard, J. (1982). *Computer use for young special needs children: An instructional guide for families and professionals.* Los Angeles: UCLA.

Franklin, K. S. (1991). Supported Employment and assistive technology. In S. L. Griffin & W. G. Revell (Eds.), *Rehabilitation counselor desktop guide to supported employment.* Richmond, VA: Rehabilitation Research Training Center on Supported Employment at Virginia Commonwealth University.

Heward, W. L., & Orlansky, M. D. (1992). *Exceptional children: An introductory survey of special education.* New York: Merrill.

McGregor, G. & Pachuski, P. (1996). Assistive technology in schools: Are teachers, ready, able, and supported. *Journal of Special Education Technology, 13*(1), 4-15.

National Center to Improve Practice. (1994). *Welcome to my preschool: Communicating with technology.* Newton, MA: Education Development Center, Inc. and WGBH Educational Foundation.

Odom, S. L., & Brown, W. B. (1993). Social interaction skills interventions for children with disabilities in integrated settings. In C. A. Peck, S. L. Odom, & D. Bricker (Eds.), *Integrating young children with disabilities into community programs: Ecological perspectives on research and implementation* (pp. 39-64). Baltimore: Paul H. Brookes.

Office of Special Education Programs. (1990). *Inquiry of Simon, 17,* EDUC. Handicapped L. Rep 225. Washington, DC: U. S. Government Printing Office.

PL 100-407 codified as 20 U.S.C. (1412 (2) Implementing regulations for state and local governments. Washington, DC: U. S. Government Printing Office.

PL 100-407 codified as 20 U.S.C. (1401(25) Implementing regulations for state and local governments. Washington, DC: U. S. Government Printing Office.

PL 100-407 codified as 20 U.S.C. (1402 (26) Implementing regulations for state and local governments. Washington, DC: U.S. Government Printing Office.

Putnam, J. W. (1993). *Cooperative learning and strategies for inclusion: Celebrating diversity in the classroom.* Baltimore: Paul H. Brookes.

RESNA Technical Assistance Project. (1992). *Assistive technology and the Individualized Education Program.* Washington, DC: RESNA Press.

U. S. Department of Education. (1996). *Eighteenth annual report to Congress on the Implementation of the Individuals with Developmental Delays Education Act.* Washington, DC: U. S. Government Printing Office.

Endnote

[1] *PL 105-17*, the most recent reauthorization of PL 94-142 was recently passed by Congress. At this time, substantive changes in IDEA have not been forthcoming with respect to issues such as inclusion or the use of technology to assist students with disabilities. Regulations will be forthcoming in the next year that will clarify the changes made in the most recent reauthorization.